Facilitating Evidence-Based, Data-Driven School Counseling

Facilitating Evidence-Based, Data-Driven School Counseling

A Manual for Practice

Brett Zyromski

Melissa A. Mariani

A Joint Publication

FOR INFORMATION:

Corwin
A SAGE Company
2455 Teller Road
Thousand Oaks, California 91320
(800) 233-9936
www.corwin.com

SAGE Publications Ltd.
1 Oliver's Yard
55 City Road
London EC1Y 1SP
United Kingdom

SAGE Publications India Pvt. Ltd.
B 1/I 1 Mohan Cooperative Industrial Area
Mathura Road, New Delhi 110 044
India

SAGE Publications Asia-Pacific Pte. Ltd.
3 Church Street
#10-04 Samsung Hub
Singapore 049483

Senior Acquisitions Editor: Jessica Allan
Senior Associate Editor: Kimberly Greenberg
Editorial Assistant: Katie Crilley
Production Editor: Melanie Birdsall
Copy Editor: Jared Leighton
Typesetter: C&M Digitals (P) Ltd.
Proofreader: Lawrence W. Baker
Indexer: Amy Murphy
Cover Designer: Anupama Krishnan
Marketing Manager: Jill S. Margulies

Printed in the United States of America

Library of Congress Cataloging-in-Publication Data

Names: Zyromski, Brett, author. | Mariani, Melissa A., author.

Title: Facilitating evidence-based, data-driven school counseling : a manual for practice / Brett Zyromski, Melissa A. Mariani.

Description: Thousand Oaks, California : Corwin, A SAGE Company, 2016. | Includes bibliographical references and index.

Identifiers: LCCN 2015040355 | ISBN 9781506323114 (pbk. : alk. paper)

Subjects: LCSH: Educational counseling—United States—Handbooks, manuals, etc.

Classification: LCC LB1027.5 .Z97 2016 | DDC 371.4/220973—dc23 LC record available at http://lccn.loc.gov/2015040355

This book is printed on acid-free paper.

16 17 18 19 20 10 9 8 7 6 5 4 3 2 1

Contents

Visit the online resource center at
http://www.corwin.com/ZyromskiEvidenceBased
for downloadable resources.

Preface

This book uses data-based decision-making strategies described in Carey Dimmitt, John C. Carey, and Trish Hatch's (2007) foundational work *Evidence-Based School Counseling: Making a Difference With Data-Driven Practices.* It is intended to be a step-by-step guide for professional school counselors to apply and to evolve to intentional, data-driven comprehensive school counseling and to use evidence-based interventions when possible. The need for this manual has been made clear not only from our own work as school counselors but also from the consultation and training we have provided to school counselor practitioners across the country and internationally. From our experience, school counselors are seeking concrete strategies to help them shift from a crisis-oriented, reactive approach to issues they face in their schools to a proactive, preventative approach. The willingness to evolve is present, but the concrete skills necessary to accomplish this shift are lacking. Our hope is that this book will provide a simple, straightforward process for successfully transitioning to an effective, intentional, and data-driven comprehensive school counseling model.

We perceive this manual as the third in a set of useful books provided by Corwin. Additional resources from other publishers do exist. However, in our opinion, Dimmitt, Carey, and Hatch's (2007) previously mentioned work, *Evidence-Based School Counseling: Making a Difference With Data-Driven Practices,* is the foundation upon which all other books and resources build as they relate to evidence-based, data-driven practices in school counseling. A more recent publication, *The Use of Data in School Counseling: Hatching Results for Students, Programs, and the Profession* by Hatch (2014), provides a thorough, comprehensive application of those tenets. This manual serves as an in-between tool. If one is interested in foundational tenets, please refer to Dimmitt, Carey, and Hatch's (2007) work, whereas if one is interested in an in-depth, comprehensive, global perspective that establishes the attitudes, knowledge, and skills needed to implement this approach, see Hatch's (2014) work. Of course, highlighting these previous two texts results in leaving many other important works unmentioned, which is not our intent.

Incredibly valuable works have also been written by others that have significantly contributed to what we now know about data-driven, evidence-based school counseling, such as Stone and Dahir's (2010) excellent *School Counselor Accountability: A MEASURE of Student Success*, which provides easy-to-understand steps for implementing an evaluation plan. In addition, Holcomb-McCoy's 2007 book, *School Counseling to Close the Achievement Gap: A Social Justice Framework for Success*, also contains many data-driven tenets. The American School Counselor Association (ASCA) is also setting its own standards for data-driven comprehensive school counseling tenets, illustrated in both their Recognized ASCA (American School Counselor Association) Model Program (RAMP; http://www.ascanationalmodel.org/learn-about-ramp) and the notable text from Kaffenberger and Young (2013), *Making Data Work* (3rd ed.). Finally, we wish to acknowledge the multitude of valuable research studies and conceptual articles that have been published in peer-reviewed, professional journals related to and supporting evidence-based, data-driven comprehensive school counseling. All of these sources have provided us with much knowledge and insight and have lent to the ideas incorporated into this book.

Acknowledgments

One of the many amazing characteristics of people in the counseling profession is their willingness to share knowledge to improve the profession and help students achieve success in life. This book is representative of the way that practices evolve through the contributions of many people across a variety of settings. A special thank you to Jay Carey and Carey Dimmitt, the director and associate director, respectively, of the Ronald H. Fredrickson Center for School Counseling Outcome Research and Evaluation and faculty at the University of Massachusetts, Amherst. Their work along with the work of Trish Hatch, the director of the Center for Excellence in School Counseling and Leadership and faculty at San Diego State University, is foundational to our understanding of evidence-based, data-driven comprehensive school counseling. They are also outstanding friends and mentors.

Many others have also helped push our understanding of how to best help students. People like Jill Cook, assistant director of the American School Counselor Association, Greg Brigman and Linda Webb, cocreators of the Student Success Skills curriculum and faculty at Florida Atlantic University and Florida State University, respectively. The evaluation chapter of this book would not have been possible without Tim Poynton's trailblazing in that area. We have been enriched by people's wisdom. Karl Squier and Pat Nailor have been generous with the wisdom of their expertise and experience. Ian Martin, Tyler Kimbel, and Elizabeth Villares make contributions to our professional expertise through every conversation we undertake together. Karen Harrington is a great partner in crime and another on the front lines of this work. Carol Dahir is endlessly generous with her time and expertise and would be an "All-American" mentor if there was such a designation.

To others who have contributed their knowledge to advance our own ability to help others, a heartfelt thanks. Stuart Chen-Hayes, Gene Eakin, Vivian Lee, Erin Mason, George McMahon, Melissa Ockerman, Chris Sink, and Carrie Wachter Morris give their professional—and often much of their personal—lives to advance our ability to better serve children and adolescents. Their support and friendship are greatly appreciated.

To the students, school counselors, and administrators who have truly helped us understand how this process works in practice every day, thank you. Olivia Ballou, Amy Beal, Angie Bielecki, Pam Boyle, Kelly Crowley, Karen Delaney, Amy Gillio, Jennifer Glass, Jacob Hornberger, Meredith Luebbers Palmer, Kendilynn Madden, Jennifer Montgomery, Brett Newton, Andrea Sebastian, Stephanie Stambaugh, Britane Swank, Liz Tackett, Erica Thomas, Carrie Wade, and Sherry Wirth continually educate us regarding evolving best practices in school counseling. This work would be impossible without them. Most of the organizational strategies in this book, those not from other authors, were created by students in classes or school counselors in workshops. Other school counselors are being left off this list but not purposefully; apologies to you who know you are partners in our work on the front line but are not listed here.

Other administrators and educational leaders truly open doors and advocate for change in our school districts in order to remove barriers to success for all students. These indefatigable warriors battle daily on multiple fronts to acquire and focus resources to help our students. Our work could not happen without them. Jay Brewer, Kathy Burkhardt, Vicki Dansberry, Angela Gabbard, Bryant Gillis, Curtis Hall, Connie Pohlgeers, Amy Razor, Jason Smith, Janice Wilkerson, and Rick Wolf have been exemplary leaders. Again, others are unintentionally left off this list. To you, we apologize. A special thank you also to Susan Cook and Jen Stansbury Koenig, two invaluable partners in this work.

To our families: You have been with us throughout our professional and personal journey. If someone is short-changed on our time or attention, it is often you. Thank you for your patience, your understanding, your support, and your faith in us and to our professional work. The foundation of any success is the love and support of those lifting you on their shoulders, and it is you who lift us on your shoulders. We hope to spend our lives returning the gift of love that you have given us. Thank you.

PUBLISHER'S ACKNOWLEDGMENTS

Corwin would like to thank the following individuals for their editorial insight and guidance:

Jennifer Betters-Bubon
Assistant Professor
University of Wisconsin–Whitewater
Whitewater, WI

Judith Bookhamer
Executive Director
Pennsylvania School Counselors Association
McKeesport, PA

Leslie Goines
Professional School Counselor
Massac County High School
Metropolis, IL

Deborah Langford
School Counselor
Houghtaling Elementary School
Ketchikan, AK

Andi Lester
Professional School Counselor
Boaz City Schools, Corley Elementary
Boaz, AL

Erin Mason
Associate Professor
DePaul University
Chicago, IL

Angela M. Mosley
Principal
Essex High School
Tappahannock, VA

Franciene Sabens
Professional School Counselor
Chester High School
Chester, IL

Diane P. Smith
School Counselor
Smethport Area School District
Smethport, PA

Joyce Stout
Elementary School Counselor
Redondo Beach Unified School District
Redondo Beach, CA

About the Authors

Brett Zyromski, PhD, is transitioning from Northern Kentucky University to join the faculty at The Ohio State University in July 2016. Dr. Zyromski is cofounder and cochair of the national Evidence-Based School Counseling Conference. He is also involved with the American School Counselor Association (ASCA) as one of eighteen Lead Recognized-ASCA-Model-Program Reviewers (LRR's) nationwide and has also served as a trainer of the ASCA National Model for the American School Counselor Association. Recently, Dr. Zyromski was a service provider for five approximately one million dollar Elementary and Secondary School Counseling Grants received by Campbell County Schools, Erlanger Independent Schools, and the Northern Kentucky Cooperative for Educational Services over the previous few years. Dr. Zyromski has published over a dozen articles related to school counseling issues and has delivered over 65 international, national, regional, and local presentations. He is a fellow at the Ronald H. Fredrickson Center for School Counseling Outcome Research and Evaluation (CSCORE). Dr. Zyromski was also the invited chair of the revision team for the Development Counseling Model for Illinois Schools.

Dr. Zyromski has consulted and trained internationally and across the United States. He has trained numerous school districts, including Chicago Public Schools, on evolving school counseling programs to evidence-based, data-driven comprehensive school counseling programs. He has provided workshops on crisis preparation and response in schools, supervision in counseling, using school counseling to change sundown town communities, and data-driven school counseling practices. Dr. Zyromski has served as an ad hoc reviewer for the journal *Professional School Counseling* and has received numerous awards and recognitions, including the 2015 Kentucky School Counselor Association Post-Secondary Counselor Award, the 2010 North Central Association for Counselor Education and Supervision Professional Leadership Award, the 2010 Illinois School Counseling Association Presidential Award, and the 2008 North Central Association for Counselor Education and Supervision Outstanding Professional Teaching Award.

Melissa A. Mariani, PhD, is an assistant professor at Florida Atlantic University (FAU) in Boca Raton, Florida, where she teaches graduate students in the School Counseling Program. Dr. Mariani has also taught at the graduate level at Nova Southeastern University. With over ten years of experience as a professional school counselor and guidance program coordinator at the elementary and middle school levels, Dr. Mariani has knowledge and experience in developing, implementing, and successfully maintaining a comprehensive school counseling program based on the American School Counselor Association's (ASCA) National Model. Her research interests include the use of evidence-based interventions, specifically those that address prosocial skill development and bullying. Promoting academic success by proactively targeting college and career readiness skills is another area of focus. Dr. Mariani has published on these topics and is a coeditor on a three-volume series of mental health encyclopedias for adolescents, *Mental Health and Mental Disorders: An Encyclopedia of Conditions, Treatments, and Well-Being*, as well, due to be released in the next year.

Dr. Mariani is passionate about professional development and has been an active board member for the Florida School Counselor Association (FSCA) for years serving as regional vice president, bylaws chair, and a member on the chapters, membership, and advocacy committees. She serves on the School Counseling Consortium for the school district of Palm Beach County and on the Advisory Committee for FAU's School Counseling Program. Dr. Mariani presents regularly at local, state, and national conferences and has served on an Expert Panel at the Evidence-Based School Counseling Conference. She is also a national trainer for the research-based, school counselor–led Student Success Skills (SSS) curriculum.

In recognition of her professional efforts, Dr. Mariani was named Florida School Counselor of the Year PK–8 in 2011 and was a semifinalist for the national award in 2012–2013 (ASCA's School Counselor of the Year). She was awarded the Outstanding Alumni Educator Award at FAU in 2012.

1 The Process

It is logical that an evidence-based, data-driven comprehensive school counseling manual be built on evidence and data outcomes. For the purpose of supporting our manual's infrastructure, outcomes from the six state studies communicated through the 2012 special edition of the *Professional School Counseling* journal are used to identify foundational constructs. **This manual is not proposing a *model* of evidence-based, data-driven comprehensive school counseling. Rather, this manual is proposing a *process* by which school counselors can quickly evolve using their current interventions to establish a data-driven comprehensive school counseling program using evidence-based interventions whenever possible.**

Evidence-based, data-driven comprehensive school counseling is not standards-based school counseling but is, rather, focused on identifying how to both provide developmentally appropriate preventative programming for all students while also prioritizing populations of inequity and offering those students evidence-based interventions. While achieving those outcomes, school counseling standards may be met as well. However, the priority when building an evidence-based, data-driven comprehensive school counseling program should be a focus on the needs of students and equity gaps as identified by data, rather than learning standards as identified by adults. Many school counselors feel comfortable with a set of standards to be met by all students. Our perspective is that if one does use standards, the standards should also be data-driven, based on evidence, and linked directly to student outcomes. A recent publication, *Achieving Excellence in School Counseling Through Motivation, Self-Direction, Self-Knowledge and Relationships* by Squier, Nailor, and Carey (2014), is the first to propose evidence-based standards for comprehensive school counseling programs. It is important to note that when the tenets mentioned above are applied, a comprehensive school counseling program meets most of the standards to qualify as a Recognized ASCA (American School Counselor Association) Model Program (RAMP), often considered the "gold standard." Thus, details related to RAMP (including a checklist detailing application requirements) and the evidence-based, data-driven process will be covered in each chapter.

As previously mentioned, the data and evidence from the 2012 special edition of the *Professional School Counseling* journal will be used to provide a template for the process. Not all research findings from the studies presented in the 2012 special edition of *Professional School Counseling* will be used, as not all are within the control of the school counselor as he or she builds a program. For example, although school counselors may advocate for a lower student-to-school-counselor ratio, it is not usually in their power to hire additional school counselors to lower that ratio. Yet four of the studies found that student-to-school-counselor ratio had significant implications for critical data elements. Further, lower student-to-school-counselor ratios resulted in improved attendance rates (Carey, Harrington, Martin, & Hoffman, 2012; Carey, Harrington, Martin, & Stevenson, 2012), improved attendance rates in high-poverty schools (Lapan, Gysbers, Stanley, & Pierce, 2012), fewer discipline issues (Carey, Harrington, Martin, & Stevenson, 2012; Lapan, Gysbers, et al., 2012), lower suspension rates (Lapan, Whitcomb, & Aleman, 2012), increased rates of attaining technical proficiency in career and vocational programs (Carey, Harrington, Martin, & Hoffman, 2012), and improved completion and graduation rates (Carey, Harrington, Martin, & Hoffman, 2012; Lapan, Gysbers, et al., 2012). Obviously, advocacy by school counselors for additional colleagues will result in significant positive outcomes for students. Other research (Carrel & Hoekstra, 2011) suggests that hiring a school counselor is more impactful on student achievement than reducing class size. In addition, having a school counselor reduces negative behaviors by approximately 20% for males and 29% for females compared to schools that did not have counselors (Carrel & Hoekstra, 2011). School counselors can have a powerful impact on student achievement, yet many of us are not equipped with the skills or tools to illustrate our impact on student behaviors and outcomes.

In order to provide an infrastructure and to identify constructs upon which to build an evidence-based, data-driven comprehensive school counseling program, the following central findings from the studies will be used:

Central Construct	Outcome	Study
The program is built upon a strong ASCA National Model orientation	Increased ACT scores, increased percentages of students taking the ACT, and enhanced student achievement in math and reading	Utah Study Carey, Harrington, Martin, & Stevenson (2012)
The school counseling program emphasizes a differentiated delivery system as prescribed by the ASCA National Model and by traditional comprehensive developmental guidance (CDG) (Gysbers & Henderson, 2012)	Decreased suspension rates, decreased discipline rates, increased attendance, and enhanced student achievement in math and reading	Nebraska Study Carey, Harrington, Martin, & Hoffman (2012)
The school counseling program uses data	Increased student achievement in math and reading, decreased suspension rates, fewer student self-reports of being teased or bullied, and increased graduation rates in vocational programs	Utah Study Carey, Harrington, Martin, & Stevenson (2012); Dimmitt, Wilkerson, & Lapan (2012)

Carey and Dimmitt (2012) provide a synopsis of implications for program building using the outcomes of the six studies:

> After a differentiated delivery system is in place, developing the mechanisms that support planning, management, and professional decision-making may become more salient factors because these mechanisms increase the effectiveness of the services actually delivered. If this interpretation is correct, it has implications for program development. In implementing an ASCA National Model program, the most effective approach may be to focus first on helping counselors develop a differentiated delivery system, then focus on

developing the mechanisms (e.g., mission statement, advisory council, decision-making processes) that guide the management of these activities. (2012, p. 147)

PURPOSE

The purpose of this book is to provide a step-by-step process for implementation of an evidence-based, data-driven comprehensive school counseling program built from the constructs of the research outcomes described above. Further, the true purpose of this book is to equip school counselors to exist and thrive within an achievement-focused environment while still primarily serving students' holistic needs. How do we, as school counselors, assert our relevance and advocate for the vital importance of serving students' nonacademic needs in an environment primarily focused on academic achievement? Thankfully, when students' needs are met—when they are healthy, safe, and feel connected—they achieve higher academic scores. Instead of shifting our professional identity, school counselors simply need to become more intentional and evaluative and then share the results of the interventions. We know what to do; we have been educated and trained to discern how best to intervene on behalf of our students. But what we lack is how to document our efforts in terms of student outcomes. Bridging the gap from "showing what we are doing" to demonstrating "how students are different as a result of what we are doing" is what is needed. Data changes often are the "coin of the realm" that we can provide to administrators and educational stakeholders who provide us a return of additional freedom to help students. Hopefully, this book will help you free the shackles of clerical work to focus on direct service and program management for students. Providing direct services to students does not mean that you release yourself from all accountability to your administrators, teachers, parents, and other stakeholders. Rather, you embrace gathering data and accountability practices realizing that these are opportunities to show others how effective you can be at impacting the lives of your students. The purpose of this book is to arm school counselors with strategies and skills to ensure they are free to help more students.

An evidence-based, data-driven comprehensive school counseling program can be built through the following steps:

1. Assessing the current school environment (see Chapter 2) as it relates to school-defined goals (as detailed in school improvement plans), as it relates to student equity gaps (as detailed in school report cards or other achievement data or achievement-related data), and as it relates

to connecting student-identified needs and student-identified barriers to success with the data previously mentioned. This data is needed both for decision-making and for designing an appropriate differentiated delivery system.

2. Setting school counseling program goals (see Chapter 3) using the data collected in Step 1. An important aspect of setting school counseling program goals is using the data collected from Step 1 to prioritize how to spend your time, targeting specific needs, which will (hopefully) result in specific outcomes. Steps 1 and 2, together, encapsulate a data-driven decision-making model, and the relationship between Steps 1 and 2 is reciprocal. That is, each step co-occurs, and one often informs the other. A logic model will be used to explain this process more clearly in Chapter 3.

3. School counseling program beliefs, mission, and vision define the direction of the program (see Chapter 4).

4. Choosing interventions strategically (evidence-based whenever possible) to meet student-identified needs (the outcomes), which consequently alter data prioritized by adults in schools (achievement data, achievement-related data, and competency-related data) (see Chapter 5). This step provides developmentally appropriate evidence-based interventions to meet students' needs. Again, the logic model is used to explain this process clearly.

5. Evaluating specific interventions (Hatch [2014] refers to this as the *flashlight approach*) to connect the intervention with outcomes. Strategies for organizing interventions using visual umbrellas and creating Excel spreadsheets for collecting data will be presented in Chapter 6. Further, strategies for evolving programs based on intervention evaluation will conclude this chapter.

6. Chapter 7 concludes the manual by connecting the evolution of the interventions to the first step of the manual—how to assess the school environment, how to evolve program goals, and how to refine the mission and vision of an evidence-based, data-driven comprehensive school counseling program.

This process is visually represented in Figure 1.1 on the next page.

We will use the process described above to "identify what needs to be addressed, which interventions or practices should be implemented, and whether the implemented intervention or practices were effective" (Dimmitt, Carey, & Hatch, 2007, p. 4).

Figure 1.1 Process for Building Evidence-Based School Counseling Program

ASSESS
- Report Card
- School Improvement Plan
- Needs Assessments
- Evaluation Results

Reciprocal Relationship

GOALS
- 2–3 per Year
- Prioritize
- Drill Down

Apply LOGIC MODEL

INTERVENTIONS
- Evidence-Based
- Targeted
- Relevant

Organize With Umbrellas

EVALUATION AND EVOLUTION
- Data Analysis
- Evolve Infrastructure

Beliefs
Mission
Vision

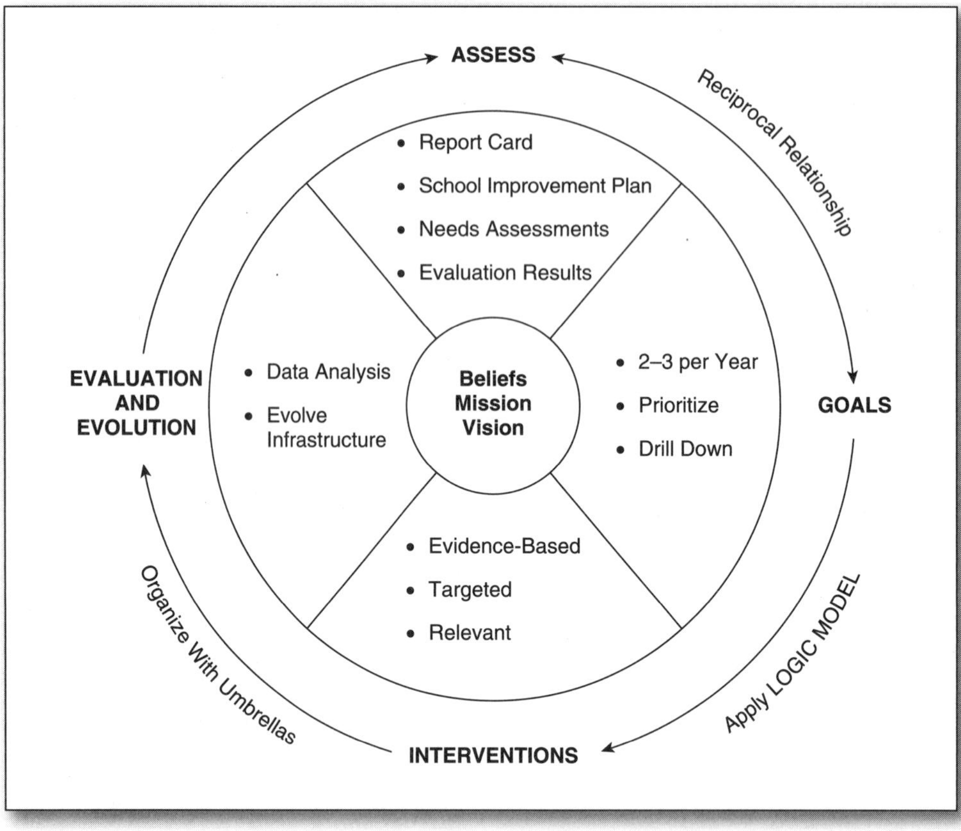

Note: The arrows indicate the reciprocal relationship of various aspects of the process.

THE ASCA NATIONAL MODEL AND EVIDENCE-BASED, DATA-DRIVEN COMPREHENSIVE SCHOOL COUNSELING

Evidence-based, data-driven comprehensive school counseling is easily organized using the American School Counselor Association's academic, career, and social/emotional domains (ASCA, 2012). An organizational structure listing school counseling program interventions by domain (umbrellas) will be introduced in Chapter 5. Further, the Recognized ASCA Model Program (RAMP) (ASCA, 2014) evaluation rubric contains many components of evidence-based, data-driven comprehensive school counseling, such as a vision statement (Item 1), mission statement (Item 2), program goals (Item 3), a school counseling curriculum action plan (Item 8) and results report (Item 9), a school counseling small-group results report (Item 10), a closing-the-gap results report (Item 11), and an overall program evaluation report (Item 12). Other items within the RAMP rubric, such as the annual agreement (Item 5) and calendars (Item 7), are valuable tools used to prioritize time and to organize implementation of evidence-based interventions throughout the school year. In addition, evidence-based, data-driven comprehensive school counseling programs create an intentional school counseling curriculum (Item 8) and intentional small-group interventions (Item 10). However, the curriculum and small groups are designed to meet student needs, as identified by students, within a logic model resulting in positive outcomes. Hence, of the twelve items included in RAMP submissions, eight are directly addressed through evidence-based, data-driven comprehensive school counseling programs, two are valuable assets to organize evidence-based, data-driven comprehensive school counseling programs, and two others are used in alternative formats within evidence-based, data-driven comprehensive school counseling programs. If the RAMP process is indicative of the focus of ASCA programs, then it is clear that making data-driven decisions and using evidence-based interventions to build a comprehensive program to remove barriers to student success is indeed a priority.

Results from the Utah and Wisconsin studies of the 2012 special edition of *Professional School Counseling* highlight the positive impacts of a more fully implemented ASCA National Model, with positive correlations with increased ACT scores, increased percentages of students taking the ACT, and enhanced student achievement in math and reading (Carey, Harrington, Martin, & Stevenson, 2012). In recent years, the ASCA has published resources to assist school counselors in data management (Kaffenberger & Young, 2013; McDougal, Graney, Wright, & Ardoin, 2010) and also provided training materials on the ASCA website to assist school counselors in managing data and choosing interventions (e.g., ASCA U's school counseling data specialist course and the Power of SMART Goals webstream) (see www.schoolcounselor.org). You must be a member to take advantage of the resources organized under the "Professional Development" and "Pubs, Periodicals, and Podcasts" sections of the ASCA website.

DEFINITIONS

The following definitions are important for understanding concepts and processes explained in this manual:

American School Counselor Association (ASCA) National Model. This refers to the third edition of a model that has evolved to provide "components of a comprehensive school counseling program" (American School Counselor Association, 2012, p. xii). The focus is on improving student achievement.

Recognized Recognized ASCA (American School Counselor Association) Model Program (RAMP). This is a designation for schools that have earned recognition from the ASCA for having a program that meets twelve components illustrating that the school counseling program aligns with the ASCA National Model. Schools must apply for the designation and submit a self-study indicating how their programs meet the twelve components detailed in the RAMP Rubric (American School Counselor Association, 2014).

Data-Driven Decision-Making. This is "a school improvement approach that uses quantitative data analysis techniques to help describe problems and to direct activities and resource allocations" (Dimmitt, Carey, & Hatch, 2007, p. 17).

Evidence-Based Interventions. Within this text, the term evidence-based interventions will be interchangeable with the term *research-based interventions*, which "refer to interventions that have evidence of effectiveness from high-quality outcome research" (Dimmitt, Carey, & Hatch, 2007, p. 49).

Comprehensive School Counseling Program. "Comprehensive in scope, preventative in design and developmental in nature," these school counseling programs focus on meeting the needs of all students through academic, career, and social/emotional programming and interventions (American School Counseling Association, 2012, p. xii).

Logic Model. This is a visual representation of a process that represents the relationship between variables or factors that lead to some outcome. It can often be a diagram or flow chart.

Umbrellas. Umbrellas are program organization tools. They are visual representations of interventions targeting issues identified using data. The interventions are organized under the three domains represented in a comprehensive school counseling program: (a) academic, (b) career, and (c) social/emotional.

Measurable. Quite simply, for the purposes of planning assessment of a school counseling intervention, one must ask, Can it be measured? Can the success or failure of the intervention be evaluated?

Results or Outcome Data. This data reflects behavior change. Related to achievement, it "reflects the academic learning and progress of students" and can include data from state achievement tests, other standardized achievement tests, SAT and ACT or other college entrance exams, algebra passing rates, grade point averages, college acceptance rates, completion rates for college-preparatory activities, advanced-placement test scores, and others (Dimmitt, Carey, & Hatch, 2007, p. 29). This data reflects how students' behaviors are leading to different outcomes, hopefully due to a combination of your interventions and others. Stone and Dahir (2010) provide an excellent list of various types of data in the appendix of *School Counselor Accountability: A MEASURE of Student Success.*

Perception Data. This type of data is useful to understand students' knowledge, attitudes, and skills (Hatch, 2014). Perception data measures "whether (a) students' attitudes or beliefs changed or shifted as a result of an activity or intervention, (b) students learned the skill (attained the competency), or (c) students' knowledge increased (Hatch, 2014, p. 75).

Process Data. This is the who, what, when, and where of data collection. This data is vital for informing others about what the school counselor did and with whom. As Hatch (2014) suggests, this data provides the who, what, when, where, and how often but *does not* address the question, So what happened as a result of the activity? (How did behaviors change? How are student different?)

Global Data. For the purposes of this manual, global data refers to data that is provided in a manner that does not relate to student level. For example, state report cards detailing how many students are achieving competency in math is global data; it does not reflect why individual students are not achieving competency. To learn the reasons a student is not achieving competency, specific data about the student is needed.

Specific Data. This is student-level data that reveals information about strengths of the student or barriers to student success. Some examples of specific data are demographics, individual results from a needs assessment, or results from participation in a focus group. Specific data is useful for intervention planning. It provides direction and focus and helps determine which intervention might be most effective. Whereas global data might let us know a problem exists, specific data will help us define the problems and explore possible solutions. It might also help us identify existing strengths upon which to build intervention.

2 Assessing the Situation

A Checklist for Assessing the Situation	
Completed?	**Processes (including any necessary materials)**
❒	Download the school improvement plan. Copy the major goals from the school improvement plan.
❒	Download the school report card. Examine each grade level carefully for equity gaps.
❒	Distribute needs assessments to every student in the school, to each teacher, to administration, and to parents.
❒	Analyze the results of the needs assessments.
❒	Combine the assessment pieces.

PURPOSE OF ASSESSING THE SITUATION

Whether you are a first-year school counselor or a counselor with twenty years of experience, the idea of evolving to a different way of doing things can be intimidating. The **first step** in the process is to stop, take a deep breath, and relax. You can do this! You already possess all the skills needed, and with the little bits of added knowledge provided in this manual, you will soon be able to illustrate how amazing you are and the impact you have on student success. In the **second step**, take a moment to think about the major interventions you currently coordinate or deliver. What is currently happening in your school? Are there current programs being coordinated (e.g., college and career readiness, cross-age peer mentoring, reality store, or test anxiety reduction)? Are classroom guidance lessons being delivered related to certain topics? Are small groups being run to address certain issues? The **third step** of our process is to assess the needs of our stakeholders. We'll show you how to do that in this chapter.

When assessing the current situation at your school, we recommend you operate from a strengths-based approach. What is already currently in place that seems to be having a positive impact? Usually, due to the current nature of school counseling, many interventions are being implemented in some manner to address perceived problems or issues in the school. Often, this is a responsive reaction to a crisis or problem that has arisen in the school that affects more than an individual student. For example, a student or some students are making it difficult for others to learn in a safe environment. Or other students are actively using drugs, or perhaps others are engaging in self-harm behaviors. Perhaps your school, like many schools, has so many student issues creating fires for the administration and for you that you feel like you are a full-time firefighter, trying to shower the school with the largest spray of water you can possibly focus on it. The strength of this approach is everyone—administration, school counselors, and teachers—feels that they are doing something to help. The weakness is that no one is quite sure if anything is helping at all, which can lead to exasperation and burnout.

Let's come back to the current moment. Take another deep breath, and remember that we are going to start with what ***is*** happening, not with what ***is not*** happening. We are going to identify equity gaps, determine what our students need, and begin to create intentional interventions to remove the barriers, as identified by student data, to their success. Soon, students' successes will create a ripple effect, much like when a rock is thrown in a lake, and this ripple effect prevents other issues from occurring. Our school counseling program can quickly grow to be the most valuable asset in the school for supporting student success. We'll have the data to show how our interventions directly lead to student achievement. *A vital aspect of this approach is to resist the pressure from the environment to start with something right away, assuming that (your mind tells you) if you start something, at least you'll be doing something. As a result, you will begin multiple programs and interventions.* This is the equivalent of throwing as many interventions against the wall as possible and hoping one or more sticks. You'll quickly find yourself juggling too many balls, and you will inevitably drop some. Furthermore, you will not know which interventions are effective and which are ineffective, as you'll have spread yourself too thin and likely wind up feeling frustrated, overwhelmed, and stressed, with burnout the end result. Instead, we are going to (a) assess the situation, (b) drill down to identify equity groups, (c) learn from the students which barriers are keeping them from being successful, (d) use interventions to target those barriers, (e) assess the impact of those interventions, and (f) evolve our interventions. Tools will be provided to accomplish each of those steps. In this chapter, we will begin by assessing the situation. To do this we need three sources of data: (a) the school improvement plan, (b) the school report card, and (c) the results of student and teacher needs assessments.

ASSESSING THE SITUATION

For your benefit, we will use actual documents from a sample middle school to illustrate the process of assessing the situation. In our online resource center (http://www.corwin.com/ZyromskiEvidenceBased), we will provide additional examples from other elementary, middle, and high schools. Each school population is distinct, but many times, normal developmental needs of students cross settings. Hopefully, our examples can illustrate both how students' normal developmental needs are shared across distinct populations as well as how each population needs us to go to them to find out their unique needs. The school improvement plan goals from the sample middle school are presented first. Then, an overview of the school report is given for the purpose of identifying equity gaps and areas for further investigation. Finally, the results of the actual needs assessments distributed, collected, and analyzed will be reviewed. The information from these sources of data will be used to determine areas to explore further in Chapter 3, when we create and define our school counseling program goals.

Notice that we are gathering distinctly different types of data. The school improvement plan reflects the focus of the school and district. It illustrates to us the "coin of the realm"—what is important to the adults. The term "coin of the realm" refers to the monetary system used in whichever culture we visit. For example, if we are in Europe, we use the euro. If we are in the United States, we use the dollar. If we are in Japan, we use the yen. If we are in Kenya, we use the shilling. And if we are in India, we use the rupee. Thus, as we move across cultures, we need to know the "coin of the realm" to understand how to trade goods and services. What is the educational "coin of the realm"? At this point in the United States, it is high-stakes testing and student achievement on those assessments, usually in the subjects of math and reading. So what are the implications for the types of data we need to collect and how we collect that data?

We need to learn how to speak the language of those in power in the educational system. That language surrounds terms such as achievement, math and reading scores, attendance, behavioral referrals, or other critical data elements. We need to know the priorities of the district because school counseling interventions that meet the needs of students, as identified by students, positively impact those critical data elements. In this process, our priority to meet the needs of students never changes. However, we will quickly improve our ability to assess the impact of our interventions and translate that impact into the language of those with power over educational systems. Evidence-based, data-driven comprehensive school counseling is not advocating for more data and less school counseling. It is actually advocating for more school counseling by illustrating the power of school counseling! The school report cards help us to accurately assess who needs our help the most, and needs assessments provide a window into student-identified needs. Only when we accurately connect interventions to student-identified needs do critical data elements change. We'll discuss that further later.

SCHOOL IMPROVEMENT PLAN

Most states require that schools submit a yearly improvement plan. School improvement plans reflect the priorities of school leadership as well as the funding priorities given to accomplishing goals. Many school improvement plan goals are created with political goals in mind, whether the goal is to satisfy the state's yearly adequate progress goal or to satisfy central-office political pressure. But the school counselor can use the school improvement plan goals to illustrate how an evidence-based, data-driven comprehensive school counseling program is achieving identified school goals. Outstanding school improvement plans are focused on removing barriers to student success, providing clear assignments and support structures to educational leaders implementing the interventions, and creating an accountability system for evaluating the success of interventions. We have provided numerous examples of school improvement plans in the onlone resource center (http://www.corwin.com/ZyromskiEvidenceBased). As mentioned above, for the purposes of this exercise, we are going to use actual documents from sample middle schools.

In many school improvement plans, the school counseling program is not mentioned, nor is the school counselor. In some cases, school counselors are mentioned related to clerical duties. In a best-case scenario (see Tichenor Middle School's school improvement plan in our online resource center), school counseling programs are mentioned as specific intervention strategies, with professional school counselors listed as the staff responsible for implementation and evaluation of the strategy. A model school improvement plan containing appropriate school counseling interventions and strategies will be presented in Chapter 7. For the purposes of this chapter, the school improvement plan needs to list the major goals (often three major goals are identified) as well as any subgoals that are related to academic achievement, career and college readiness, or social/emotional issues. Any existing school counseling interventions that serve as school improvement plan strategies (see Figure 2.1) also need to be listed. **School improvement plans can be long and confusing. All you need to pull for the assessment stage are the major goals.**

Goals within a school improvement plan are often presented in a table, as are school improvement plan strategies (see Figure 2.1). However, we do not need to gather all the components listed within the table, only the goals stated in numerical terms. What we see in Figure 2.1 is a summary of the three major goals listed in the school improvement plan.

As mentioned above, for the purposes of school counseling program goal setting, only goals need to be collected. One of the three major goals, as stated in the example school improvement plan above, is related to improving math and reading scores. A second goal is to increase the number of students scoring "college and career ready"—a designation used by various states, including the state of Kentucky, to qualify when students pass certain standardized evaluations. The third goal is to improve reading and math proficiency ratings for nonduplicated gap groups, such as students with identified disabilities or receiving free or reduced lunch. Notice that the goals are data oriented. The goals are not stated in operationalized terminology. The goal is a global data goal, not a specific data goal. We can use these goals to illustrate the impact of our school counseling program.

For the purposes of our exercise, write these three goals down somewhere. They will be used later in the chapter. The three major school improvement plan goals are as follows:

1. Increase the averaged combined reading and math K-PREP scores for middle school students from 44% to 72% by 2017.
2. Increase the percentage of students who are college and career ready from 51.6% to 68% by 2015.
3. Increase the average combined reading and math proficiency ratings for all students in nonduplicated gap group from 42.2% to 66.5% in 2017.

Notice the achievement goals are all for 2017; when it was created, this school improvement plan was a five-year plan. The school improvement plan included yearly subgoals. We will create a list of both and learn how to use that list of school improvement plan goals and subgoals to create our own school counseling program goals in Chapter 3.

Figure 2.1 An Example of School Improvement Goals: Summary of a Sample Middle School

#	Goal Name	Goal Details	Goal Type	Measurable Objective	Total Funding
1	Increase the averaged combined reading and math K-PREP scores for middle school students from 44% to 72% by 2017.	Objectives: 1 Strategies: 4 Activities: 7	Organizational	Collaborate to increase the overall reading and math scores for the middle school from 44.3 to 49.9 by 10/21/2013 as measured by scored K-PREP results.	$0
2	Increase the percentage of students who are college and career ready from 51.6% to 68% by 2015.	Objectives: 1 Strategies: 2 Activities: 2	Organizational	Collaborate to increase the percentage of students who are college and career ready by 10/18/2013 by Explore results.	$1,400
3	Increase the average combined reading and math proficiency ratings for all students in nonduplicated gap group from 42.2% to 66.5% in 2017.	Objectives: 1 Strategies: 2 Activities: 3	Organizational	Collaborate to increase the math and reading proficiency in math and reading gap groups by 10/18/2013 as measured by K-PREP scores.	$6,000

Note: K-PREP is the standardized end of grade assessment used in Kentucky. Other states have similar end-of-grade assessment tools. Also, be sure to define what the nonduplicated gap groups are in your school improvement plan (e.g., ability, socioeconomic status, gender, and ethnicity).

ACHIEVEMENT OR ACHIEVEMENT-RELATED DATA: SCHOOL REPORT CARD

Schools are mandated by No Child Left Behind (NCLB) legislation to report achievement to state offices of education. Although some states have recently altered the level to which they are implementing No Child Left Behind legislation, most states have data-reporting systems indicating academic progress made by individual schools in the state, as scored on standardized evaluation instruments. The purpose of using school report card information is to identify achievement gaps or other equity gaps to incorporate into school counseling program goals. The data within the report cards is global data, not student-level data. The report card can tell you that students are not achieving compared to peers around the state, but the report card cannot tell you why the students are not achieving. Many people spend hours examining global data in an attempt to data mine it for clues as to issues for their students. You will not find the clues to why your students are struggling in global data. You need specific data to determine why your students are struggling. We use global data—the data from school report cards—to learn about equity gaps and identify patterns and indicators that problems exist. However, to learn about barriers to success or why students are not achieving compared to their peers, we need specific data (student-level data). We'll go further into depth regarding specific data when we discuss needs assessments later. For now, let's examine global data to determine equity gaps and discuss the implications.

In the state of Kentucky, one can access school report cards using the Kentucky School Report Card website at applications.education.ky.gov/SRC. To access Ohio School Report Cards, go to reportcard.education.ohio.gov/Pages/default.aspx. To access Florida School Report Cards, go to schoolgrades.fldoe.org. To access Oregon School Report Cards, go to www.ode.state.or.us/search/results/?id=116. These websites were discovered by simply inserting the state and then the words "school report cards" into the Google search engine. Once you have learned how to access your own school's report card, you can search it for equity gaps. We will continue to use sample middle schools for our exercise throughout this chapter.

When first looking at a report card, it can be confusing. We suggest you sit down with school administration to review your report card. School administrators are often experts at examining their school report card and identifying gaps in achievement. For the purpose of our exercise, we are going to look at only math and reading achievement across sixth, seventh, and eighth grades at sample middle schools. In Kentucky, achievement is measured using four categories: (a) percent novice, (b) percent apprentice, (c) percent proficient, and (d) percent distinguished. High-achieving students will score at distinguished levels.

Remember to look at the year in which students performed on your report card. It often takes a state an entire year to publish school report cards. As a result, the data is immediately outdated. So how is it useful? It can be used to capture persistent equity gaps. Report cards illustrate patterns of differences in achievement between groups. They also provide school counselors with a direction to investigate—to drill down from global data to specific data. They provide us with a first step to take in our investigation into how we should organize our priorities to align with the school's priorities. Remember, we know from the school improvement plan that achievement in math and reading is a priority for the school. We can help the school accomplish that goal without focusing on math and reading. Here is how: Usually, when a student struggles academically, research suggests it is because of issues in *motivation, self-direction, self-knowledge,* or *relationships* (Squier, Nailor, & Carey, 2014). One way to think about it is the difference between *seat time* and *engaged seat time*. A student could sit in a seat for twelve hours a day and not learn much. A student must be engaged in the education process while sitting in that seat to learn. School counselors are uniquely qualified in schools to help students improve their motivation, self-direction, self-knowledge, and relationships. When students increase their motivation or increase their self-knowledge, internalize self-direction, and have healthy relationships, students are freed to focus and engage more deeply in their academics. Further, when school counselors use data to inform their programmatic decisions, it results in increased student achievement in math and reading, a decrease in suspension rates, fewer students reporting being bullied or teased, and increased graduation rates in vocational programs (Carey, Harrington, Martin, & Stevenson, 2012; Dimmitt, Wilkerson, & Lapan, 2012).

The school report card for our example middle school reveals equity gaps that exist between males and females in seventh grade in both math and reading. How did we identify the gap? See Table 2.1. The table shows that in math, 45.3% of males scored at proficient or distinguished (33.7% scored at proficient plus 11.6% scored at distinguished), compared to 36.1% of females scoring at proficient or distinguished (26.5% at proficient plus 9.6% at distinguished), resulting in a 9.2% gap between the percentage of males scoring at proficient or distinguished compared to females. Half of our females in seventh grade (50.6%) are scoring at the apprentice achievement level in math. For the purposes of this exercise, we will treat these seventh graders as if they are now in eighth grade. It is critical to know their grade at present to accurately connect the results of needs assessments to the equity gaps.

A second equity gap identified by the seventh-grade report card is the percentage of students scoring at distinguished who receive free or reduced-cost meals. Inequity related to income is common. Compared to the percentage

Table 2.1 Sample Middle School, Grade 7

Accountability - Achievement - Mathematics - Middle School - Grade 07 - Performance Level																		
	Number Accountable 100 days Enrolled			Percent Novice			Percent Apprentice			Percent Proficient			Percent Distinguished			Percent Proficient/ Distinguished		
Level	School	District	State	School	District	State	School	District	State	School	District	State	School	District	State	School	District	State
All Students	178	178	50,815	14.6	14.6	17.2	44.4	44.4	44.2	30.3	30.3	30.7	10.7	10.7	7.8	41.0	41.0	38.6
Male	95	95	26,230	15.8	15.8	19.5	38.9	38.9	42.8	33.7	33.7	29.6	11.6	11.6	8.1	45.3	45.3	37.7
Female	83	83	24,582	13.3	13.3	14.7	50.6	50.6	45.7	26.5	26.5	32.0	9.6	9.6	7.6	36.1	36.1	39.6
White (Non-Hispanic)	–	–	41,254	14.9	14.9	14.9	44.3	44.3	43.4	29.9	29.9	33.2	10.9	10.9	8.5	40.8	40.8	41.7
African American	***	***	5,550			33.0			49.4			15.8			1.7			17.6
Hispanic	***	***	1,902			21.5			51.1			23.6			3.8			27.4
Asian	***	***	687			8.7			27.1			33.6			30.6			64.2
American Indian or Alaska Native			152			17.8			45.4			32.2			4.6			36.8
Native Hawaiian or Other Pacific Islander			37			24.3			35.1			29.7			10.8			40.5
Two or more races			1,115			20.7			48.5			25.7			5.0			30.8
Migrant			112			23.2			53.6			22.3			0.9			23.2
Limited English Proficiency			904			36.6			48.2			13.2			2.0			15.2
Free/Reduced-Price Meals	102	102	29,653	20.6	20.6	23.5	47.1	47.1	49.9	29.4	29.4	23.2	2.9	2.9	3.4	32.4	32.4	26.6
Disability-With IEP (Total)	19	19	5,692	31.6	31.6	43.7	47.4	47.4	42.2	21.1	21.1	11.8	0.0	0.0	2.3	21.1	21.1	14.1
Disability-With IEP (not including Alternate)	–	–	5,170	33.3	33.3	45.8	50.0	50.0	41.5	16.7	16.7	10.7	0.0	0.0	2.0	16.7	16.7	12.7
Disability-With Accommodation (not including Alternate)	–	–	3,919	25.0	25.0	47.0	56.3	56.3	41.5	18.8	18.8	9.9	0.0	0.0	1.7	18.8	18.8	11.6
Disability-Alternate Only	***	***	522			22.6			49.0			22.8			5.6			28.4
Gap Group (non-duplicated)	106	106	32,153	20.8	20.8	23.6	47.2	47.2	49.7	29.2	29.2	23.2	2.8	2.8	3.5	32.1	32.1	26.7

Notice the difference between the percentage of males and females scoring at distinguished compared to the percentage of students receiving free or reduced price meals.

Notice the difference between the percentage of males and females scoring at proficient/distinguished. An equity gap exists.

Note: Percentages may not sum to 100% due to rounding. School results are based on the grades in the school. District and state results are based on the standard grade configuration of K–5, 6–8, and 9–12.
"***" indicates unreportable populations with fewer than 10 students or populations where all students score at the same performance level.
"—" indicates that counts are suppressed to protect student identification required by the Family Educational Rights and Privacy Act (FERPA).

of males (11.6%) and females (9.6%) scoring at distinguished, only 2.9% of students receiving free or reduced-cost meals are scoring at the distinguished level. If we look at which levels of achievement the majority of these students score, we see that 67.7% of the students in the school receiving free or reduced-cost meals score at either novice or apprentice levels. These students are clearly struggling with barriers to their success. We can prioritize investigating into the barriers for this population.

We will stop our analysis of the school report card at this point. It should be noted that our example middle school happens to be a rural school with little ethnic variation. At this point, we have identified two equity gaps. We can now take steps to investigate further into the current status of our eighth-grade females and students receiving free or reduced meals. If we repeat this process by looking at the sixth-grade scores on the report card, we will find additional equity gaps that we can use to drive additional investigation. These investigations drill down from the global-data level to specific data regarding why students are struggling to be successful. This is a vital step—***do not skip the drill-down step.*** We must investigate to identify the ecological, interpersonal, and intrapersonal issues faced by these students. *Also—and this is vital—we must investigate to learn about the strengths of these populations and what they are currently doing to achieve their present level of success. We can often support their current strengths to increase their success.*

NEEDS ASSESSMENTS

For the purpose of this example, the actual needs assessment results from sample middle schools will be used to complete the exercise. However, additional examples of needs assessments are provided in the online resource center (http://www.corwin.com/ZyromskiEvidenceBased). We suggest always editing and adjusting needs assessments to assess the unique issues at your school. Attempt to keep your needs assessments to two pages or less. Do not distribute needs assessments to kindergarten or first-grade students. You can consult with those teachers. Or it is possible to conduct a story-based needs assessment with students in kindergarten and first grade. Read a story related to normal developmental issues, and ask students to share stories of times they experienced similar issues. Students in kindergarten and first grade love to share stories, and you can take notes about abnormal developmental issues, excessive conflict, or other issues the students experience on the playground, on the buses, in the classroom, or at home. Do not neglect to collect strengths and issues faced by students in kindergarten or first grade. Hearing the students' voices is a vital component of providing intentional services that help student development and success.

Often, needs assessments can be transferred to a digital format using SurveyMonkey or other online survey tools such as Google Docs. Some school districts own their own online survey tools for other reasons; be sure to check with the central office. Distributing and collecting needs assessments electronically saves a lot of time and effort. Usually, the online survey tool, such as SurveyMonkey or Google Docs, has analysis capabilities built into the survey tool. Hence, the logistical issues of passing our physical copies to 1,200 students are alleviated by having students take ten minutes to complete them in a computer lab, and the analysis burden is alleviated by the built-in capabilities of the online survey tool. One last note regarding needs assessments: Whenever possible, have a school counselor lead the needs assessment survey and walk the students through each item. This increases the fidelity of the needs assessment process. Teachers are burdened by many surveys, and unfortunately, at times, the needs assessment can become "one more thing" faced by teachers. If students do not carefully consider each item, we cannot trust the results. This affects the validity of the self-report data.

The needs assessment used to collect this data is included in Appendix C, as are results for each grade and the entire school. Results from teachers are also included. Interestingly, teachers and students agree regarding the needs of students about 60% to 70% of the time. This is a significant difference in opinion. For example, at one high school, a majority of the teachers identified poverty as a major issue facing students. However, only two students out of the entire student population marked poverty as an issue facing students. Students worked one or two jobs to make money; they had grown up in poverty and lived with poverty. This is not to say poverty is not a barrier to success for these students. Research tends to consistently show that poverty is a major barrier to success. However, these students did not perceive poverty as a barrier to their success. Hence, efforts were focused on barriers identified by students, and the school experienced a quick increase in the number of student scoring at college or career ready on state achievement tests.

To correlate the results of our needs assessments with the equity gaps identified in the report card, we will first look specifically at female eighth-grade students to determine which issues they identified as barriers to their success. Current eighth-grade females report the following major issues:

- Bullying or harassment (62.0% of those polled list this as a concern)
- Rumors and gossip (50.4% of those polled list this as a concern)
- Hurting or cutting oneself (42.6% of those polled list this as a concern)
- Feeling sad or depressed a lot (42.6% of those polled list this as a concern)
- Fights or coping with stress (34.9% of those polled list this as a concern)

It seems that the females at the example middle school do not feel comfortable or safe interpersonally at school. Intrapersonal issues are also identified. The school counselor can intervene to help students with these concerns. Choosing interventions to help with these issues is a vital part of the process. Setting goals to target these issues while still fulfilling the school improvement plan goals is also important. We will learn how to set appropriate goals in the next chapter.

COMBINING THE ASSESSMENT PIECES

Once the three pieces of information have been collected, they can be examined for themes, equity gaps, and areas of intervention. A synopsis can be created of our initial assessment of one grade level (see Figure 2.2 on the next page).

To review what we know thus far in our assessment process, consider the following:

- We know that the school emphasizes math and reading achievement. We know the school emphasizes college and career readiness as evaluated by assessments.
- We know that equity gaps in achievement exist between females and males. We also know students receiving free or reduced-cost meals scored lower on the achievement tests.
- We know that females are struggling with feeling safe at school, with interpersonal relationships, and with intrapersonal issues.

In the next chapter, we will apply this knowledge to create two school counseling goals.

FULFILLING COMPONENTS OF RAMP

The Recognized ASCA Model Program (RAMP) requires that school counselors write narratives about how each of the twelve components are fulfilled. These narratives must be rich and detailed with clear explanations about why certain components are included and excluded. The process of assessing the current situation described in this chapter is going to inform the creation of school counselor beliefs (part of Item 1: Vision Statement), mission (Item 2), vision (Item 1), and program goals (Item 3) and will eventually help guide which small groups are developed (Item 10), which equity gaps are targeted (Item 11), and which interventions and programs were chosen to target theses issues. This chapter provides the foundation upon

Figure 2.2 Combining the Assessment Pieces

School Improvement Plan Goals	Report Card Themes or Gaps	Results of Needs Assessments
Increase combined reading and math K-PREP scores for middle school students from 44% to 72% by 2017.	Seventh-grade females (current eighth graders) present a significant equity gap in math achievement compared to males. Seventh-grade students receiving free or reduced-cost meals (current eighth graders) present a significant equity gap in math compared to students not receiving free or reduced-cost meals.	Current eighth-grade females report the following major issues: • *Bullying or harassment* (62.0% of those polled list this as a concern) • *Rumors and gossip* (50.4% of those polled list this as a concern) • *Hurting or cutting oneself* (42.6% of those polled list this as a concern) • *Feeling sad or depressed a lot* (42.6% of those polled list this as a concern) • *Fights or coping with stress* (34.9% of those polled list this as a concern)
Increase percentage of students who are college and career ready from 51.6% to 68% by 2015. (*Note:* Since this is assessed through student scores on achievement tests, increasing math and reading scores and closing math and reading gaps will also help meet this schoolwide goal.)	Seventh-grade females (current eighth graders) present a significant equity gap in math achievement compared to males. Seventh-grade students receiving free or reduced-cost meals (current eighth graders) present a significant equity gap in math compared to students not receiving free or reduced-cost meals.	Current eighth-grade females report the following major issues: • *Bullying or harassment* (62.0% of those polled list this as a concern) • *Rumors and gossip* (50.4% of those polled list this as a concern) • *Hurting or cutting oneself* (42.6% of those polled list this as a concern) • *Feeling sad or depressed a lot* (42.6% of those polled list this as a concern) • *Fights or coping with stress* (34.9% of those polled list this as a concern)
Increase the average combined reading and math proficiency ratings for all students in nonduplicated gap groups from 42.2% to 66.5% in 2017.	Seventh-grade students receiving free or reduced-cost meals (current eighth graders) present a significant equity gap in math compared to students not receiving free or reduced-cost meals.	Current eighth-grade females report the following major issues: • *Bullying or harassment* (62.0% of those polled list this as a concern) • *Rumors and gossip* (50.4% of those polled list this as a concern) • *Hurting or cutting oneself* (42.6% of those polled list this as a concern) • *Feeling sad or depressed a lot* (42.6% of those polled list this as a concern) • *Fights or coping with stress* (34.9% of those polled list this as a concern)

Note: Figure 2.2 represents three assessment pieces to use to make data-driven decisions regarding student needs and equity gaps.

which everything else is built. The annual agreement (Item 5) will reflect the priorities created by focusing on these groups of students and by choosing interventions to remove barriers to their success. Calendars (Item 7) will be created, reflecting the time put into programming, classroom guidance, and small-group interventions targeting the needs of these students. If the intervention is a schoolwide intervention, then the school counseling curriculum (Item 8) will reflect that focus and the evaluation components (Item 9 and Item 12) will also reflect the success of these interventions.

3 Setting Goals

A Checklist for Setting Goals	
Completed?	**Processes (including any necessary materials)**
❐	Start with the "Combining the Assessment Pieces" document.
❐	Use the logic model.
❐	Insert data indicators into the logic model.
❐	Drill down from global data to specific data, then insert it into the logic model.
❐	Set goals. Be sure to be specific about who, what, and how.
❐	Use the SMART goals template.
❐	Keep the partially complete logic model, and move to examining possible evidence-based interventions (or current programs or interventions).

PURPOSE OF SETTING GOALS

Setting goals is vital to organize the structure of the school counseling program and to prioritize how school counselors spend their time. Too often, school counselors are on a downward spiral toward burnout within the first three years of their entry into the profession because they are overwhelmed with the demands of the position. However, the demands of the position are often predefined by the administration or expectations based on the job roles of the previous school counselor. As we have traveled around the United

States providing training and consultations, we have noticed a few consistent themes emerge: (a) school counselors often feel stuck in job roles not related to their professional identity (e.g., testing and assessment coordinator or director of special education meetings), (b) school counselors are afraid to say no to existing inappropriate job roles or new requests from administration for fear of losing their jobs, and (c) school counselors are either not equipped with the skills to advocate for and evolve to more appropriate job roles, or they are apprehensive to take the initial step.

We have some good news and some bad news. Here is the bad news first: Fear is situational and immediate. It paralyzes and often narrows a person's focus to the present time and place. However, it is important to take a more global perspective. If we do not advocate for job role changes, we may lose our jobs—and not just our own jobs personally. Others will end up losing theirs too. In other words, if you do not act to advocate for a more defined, comprehensive school counseling role, the chances are you will eventually lose your job. This is a harsh reality of our economy and achievement-focused political environment. Already, in some states, guidance counselors have been replaced with deans of students, behavioral interventionists, response-to-intervention specialists, and administrative assistants. If a person is a quasi-administrator and clerical specialist and is being paid a masters-plus-experience salary, would it not make fiscal sense to replace that person with a dean of students paid at an undergraduate pay scale? Furthermore, unfortunately, we've personally worked with excellent school counselors who did not advocate for their positions using data because they felt safe with their administration, in that they had "good" relationships with their principals. Then, when their administrators took jobs elsewhere in order to advance their own careers, these counselors were no longer on stable ground and they ended up leaving or being replaced the following school year.

Now, here is the good news: This manual provides you the tools you need to illustrate how amazing you are, how impactful your program is, and how your time needs to be prioritized in direct service to students whenever possible. When we talk with district administrators and school administrators, we do not advocate for additional school counselors or evolved job roles of school counselors using process data. Process data is the data that tells us how many groups we led, with which students, about which topics, and when we led those groups. In the current achievement-focused political environment, that type of data will not provide you any leverage to evolve your job role. We immediately ask administrators, Would you like a school counseling program that raises math and reading scores, increases college and career readiness, increases attendance, and reduces dropouts? We have never had an administrator say no to that question. Achievement is the coin of the realm, and we need to learn to trade in that currency. Fortunately, school counseling interventions, when accurately focused on removing barriers to the success of students, often lead to achievement-related data change. We'll clarify this in the coming chapters and provide you both examples and process for sharing your own impactful results.

Setting goals in this chapter will focus on helping school counselors create a streamlined accountability system that is low maintenance and produces outcomes each year that can be shared with stakeholders and used to evolve programming. Further, setting goals will help the school counselor prioritize how to spend his or her time, focus more closely on reducing the inequities uncovered in the data, and identify the next steps toward targeting interventions that will make a positive impact on students' achievement (Holcomb-McCoy, 2007). As we mentioned in the beginning of the book, the infrastructure of the process is founded on research.

As we create our goals, we will look ahead to interventions that are differentiated, multilevel, and comprehensive in nature (whenever possible) (Carey & Dimmitt, 2012), and we will found our goals on the data we uncovered through our assessment process (detailed in the previous chapter).

Central Construct	Outcome	Study
The school counseling program emphasizes a differentiated delivery system as prescribed by the ASCA National Model and by traditional comprehensive developmental guidance (CDG; Gysbers & Henderson, 2012).	Decreased suspension rates, decreased discipline rates, increased attendance, and enhanced student achievement in math and reading	Nebraska Study Carey, Harrington, Martin, and Hoffman (2012)
The school counseling program must use data.	Increased student achievement in math and reading, decreased suspension rates, fewer student self-reports of being teased or bullied, and increased graduation rates in vocational programs	Utah Study Carey, Harrington, Martin, and Stevenson (2012) Dimmitt, Wilkerson, and Lapan (2012)

DATA-DRIVEN DECISION-MAKING

In the previous chapter, a three-pronged approach to collecting and assessing data was provided. Only one example and only one process were shared purposefully because, in our experience, school counselors are often overwhelmed by the many various approaches to data collection and analysis. However, it is important that school counselors are aware that although we use math and reading data in our example, many types of data exist to use when formulating our goals. Dahir and Stone (2012) describe these as "Critical Data Elements" (p. 228). Other authors (Dimmitt, Carey, & Hatch, 2007; Hatch, 2014; Holcomb-McCoy, 2007; Kaffenberger & Young, 2013, among others) as well as the ASCA National Model (2012) all detail various types of critical data elements. We list the data elements (see Dahir & Stone, 2012) by whether or not the data captures behavior change.

The ASCA (2012; Kaffenberger & Young; 2013) categorizes data three ways: (a) process data, (b) perception data, and (c) outcome (or results) data. Hatch (2014) describes process data as the "what you did for whom" data (p. 74). This type of data tells a story about what happened, for whom it happened, when it happened, and where and how often it happened. This is the "bean counting" of data collection. A sentence providing process data might be as follows: Two groups of eighth-grade females (who) received eight weeks of Student Success Skills small-group intervention (what) once a week (when) during the fall from the school counselor in the school counselor's office (where and how). This type of data is vital to provide foundational understanding about what services, programs, and interventions students are receiving.

The next category of data is perception data. Hatch (2014) describes perception data as data that tell us "what a student thinks, knows, or can demonstrate as a result of a lesson or activity" (p. 75). Perception data collects information about students' attitudes, knowledge, and skills (Hatch, 2014). Attitudes and beliefs can be assessed using pre- and post-surveys or tests. We'll describe pre- and post-tests in further detail in Chapter 6, the chapter dedicated to evaluation and evolution of school counseling interventions and programming. One of my (Zyromski) favorite examples to use regarding perception data is an example related to interventions designed to decrease bullying. A pre- and post-survey assessing attitudes and knowledge of students related to bullying might assess the following (just to name a few examples): (a) students' attitudes related to reporting cyber-harassment, (b) students' knowledge of what it means to be a bystander, and (c) students' knowledge regarding characteristics of bullying behavior.

Table 3.1 lists some of these data elements. One would hope that students' perceptions and knowledge related to the above items would change from before they received the school counseling intervention to after they received the intervention. Assessing changes in attitudes and knowledge is important to understand how well we are designing and conducting our interventions. However, the true testament to whether the bullying material was internalized and applied is *behavior change*. Behavior change can be assessed either through an assessment of how skills develop as a result of our intervention or through outcome data.

Table 3.1 Categories of Data With Examples

Categories	Types of Data
Data reflecting behavior change	Test results Grade point averages Armed Services Vocational Aptitude Battery (ASVAB) test results Standardized achievement tests (especially if given multiple times in the same calendar year) Attendance Rank in class Enrollment in AP courses Enrollment in other programs (honors, International Baccalaureate, or college level) Exceptional student education screening and placement Number of credits passed Discipline rate (classroom data or office referrals) Suspension rate Alcohol, tobacco, and other drug violations Grade-level achievement in math, reading, or other subjects Parent or guardian involvement data Participation rate in extracurricular activities Homework completion rates Four-year graduation plan completion rate Scholarship application completion rate College application completion rate

Categories	Types of Data
Data reflecting changes in attitudes or knowledge	Pre-post tests on competencies, knowledge, or attitudes related to an intervention
Process data	What, when, where and how, and for whom
Demographics	Ethnicity Gender Free or reduced-cost meals Other socioeconomic measures Housing Family with active military Grade level Age Single-parent households Other household information Language spoken at home Teacher assignment Ability or disability

Note: Table 3.1 provides examples of demographic data, process data, perception data, and results data.

Using our bullying curriculum example above, let's imagine that prior to the intervention a student did not respond that it was important to report cyberbullying, did not know what it looked like to be a bystander, and could not identify characteristics of bullying behaviors. Fortunately, after our intervention, the student marked that it was very important to report cyberbullying, identified bystander behavior and steps for getting friends together to help end bullying in hallways, and could identify characteristics of bullying behaviors. Our intervention, according to our perception data, was a success! Unfortunately, after class, this same student went down the hallway pushing every fifth student into the lockers, just to get laughs from his friends. Oops. The student possessed all the knowledge needed but did not change her behavior, so would we still call our intervention a success? We suggest the priority be put on collecting data that measures behavior change. Collect pre- and post-survey data when needed, but during planning, be sure to focus on identifying which data can be collected that will reflect behavior change.

Outcome data related to the bullying intervention example provided above could be attendance data (as research shows that students skip school to avoid harassment), office referrals (tricky data point—more on that in Chapter 6), teacher behavior reports, grade point average data, and test results. You may wonder how data points not directly related to bullying can indicate change. When students feel safe in school, they engage in the educational process, which will naturally lead to higher achievement. A visual representation of this process will be provided later. However, simply stated, for the purposes of goal setting, we need to focus on using data that reflects behavior change whenever possible. *The most useful assessments for us to use are those that happen multiple times within the same school year.*

A FINAL NOTE ON DATA: DATA COLLECTED ANNUALLY

Some types of achievement data were not included above that school districts value highly. It is not that collecting this data is not important. However, it is important to use data that we can correlate directly to our school counseling interventions. The easiest data to use to do that is data that is collected multiple times in the same academic year. However, we can also use data that is collected annually to show important patterns over time that were positively impacted by the school counseling program. State comprehensive exams; the Preliminary Scholastic Achievement Test (PSAT); the SAT; the ACT; other standardized achievement tests; dropout rates from year to year; post-secondary matriculation rates to technical schools, other two-year institutions, or four-year institutions or service in the military; retention rates; and patterns regarding the percentage of students achieving something from year to year are all valuable data points. We will touch on how to design your school counseling evaluation process to collect these points of data as well as data that reflects behavior change within the same school year in Chapter 6.

USING A LOGIC MODEL

Now that we understand all the various types of data we can use when setting our goals, we can proceed in defining our goal based on the information we have gathered during the assessment phase of the process. Here is a review:

- We know that the school emphasizes math and reading achievement. We know the school emphasizes college and career readiness as evaluated by assessments.

- We know that equity gaps in achievement exist between females and males. We also know students receiving free or reduced-cost meals scored lower on the achievement tests.
- We know that females are struggling with feeling safe at school, with interpersonal relationships, and with intrapersonal issues.

The logic model in Figure 3.1 was adapted, with permission, from Dimmitt, Carey, and Hatch's (2007) Data-Based Decision Making Logic Model (p. 25). It reflects a process through which school counselors can input data indicators, drill down to identify equity gaps and target populations, define appropriate evidence-based interventions (whenever possible), describe logistics, and plan evaluation and evolution.

Please note that the seven steps in the logic model mirror the topics of each of the chapters within this book. We'll go step by step through completing the

Figure 3.1 The Evidence-Based School Counseling Logic Model

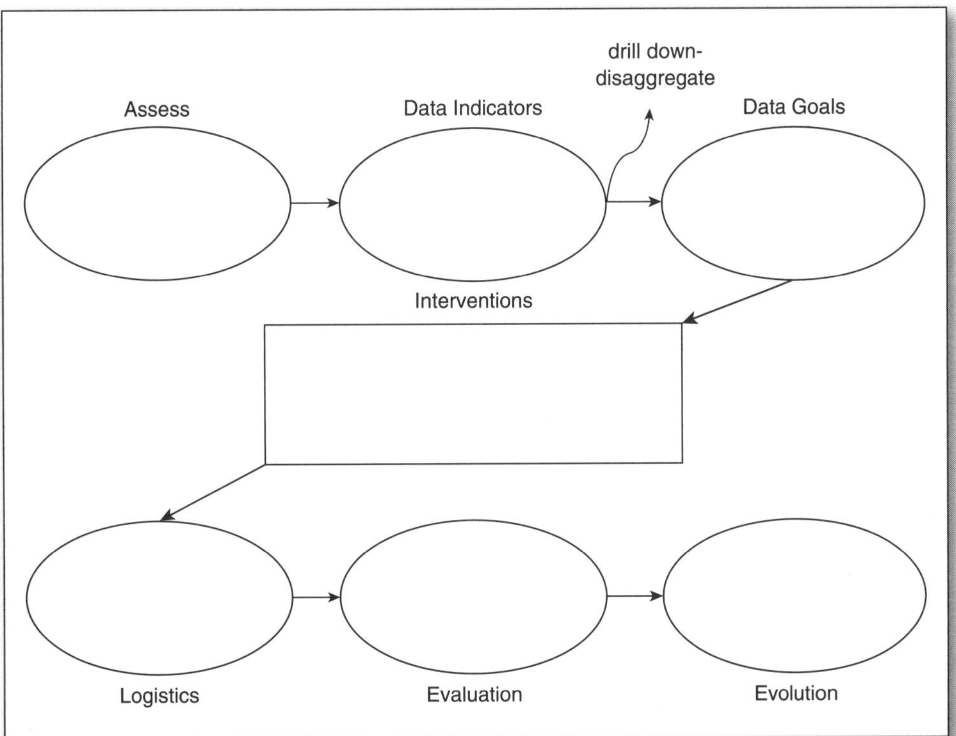

Source: Adapted from Dimmitt, Carey, & Hatch (2007).

Note: Figure 3.1 represents a logic model to use to make decisions about school counseling interventions to meet student needs and change critical data results.

logic model with the information we have gathered thus far in the process. Figure 3.2 shows how we began the logic model process by listing the data indicators that first caught our attention. Math and reading scores were prioritized by the school as areas of focus.

Figure 3.2 Logic Model With Data Indicators

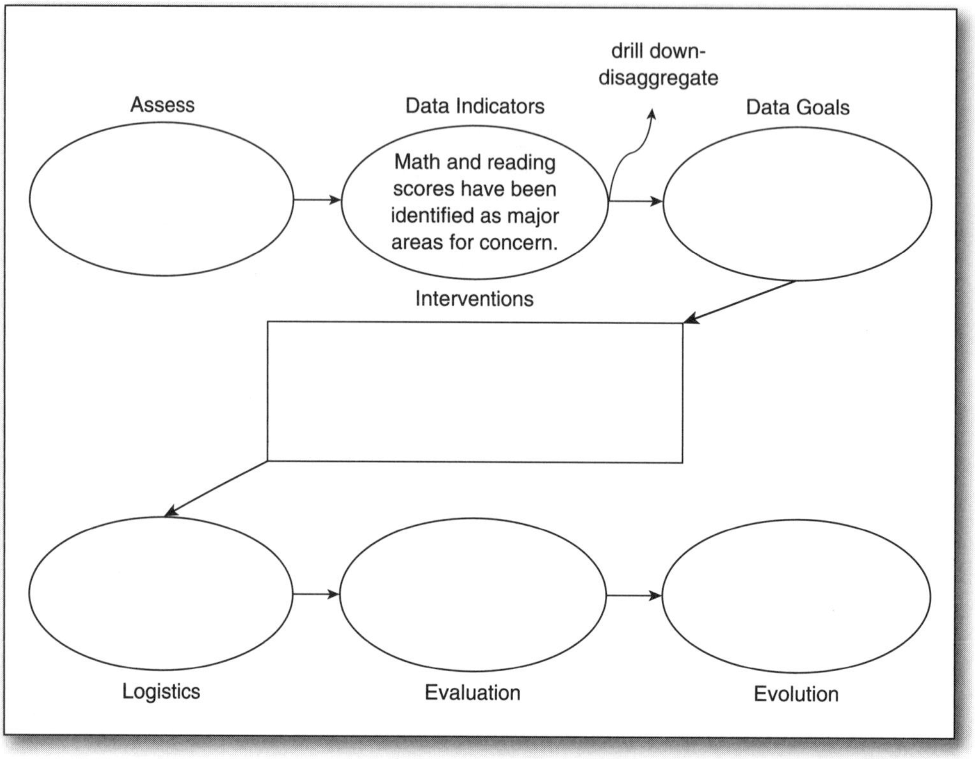

Source: Adapted from Dimmitt, Carey, & Hatch (2007).

Note: Figure 3.2 represents the logic model with an example of a data indicator included.

DRILLING DOWN: GLOBAL VERSUS SPECIFIC DATA

As we previously reviewed, having global data indicating there is a problem with math or reading achievement does not tell us much about what is keeping our specific students from high scores in math or reading. We will take two steps to figure out exactly what the issues are that we need to address. The first of the two steps is to drill down deeper, again moving from global data to specific data. We did that in our assessment when we looked more closely at the school report card in order to identify equity gaps. Drilling down further identified that our females were struggling in math as compared to our males. We also learned that students receiving free or reduced-cost meals struggled in math as compared to their peers not receiving free or reduced-cost meals. Let's insert that data into our logic model (see Figure 3.3).

Figure 3.3 Logic Model With Disaggregated Data

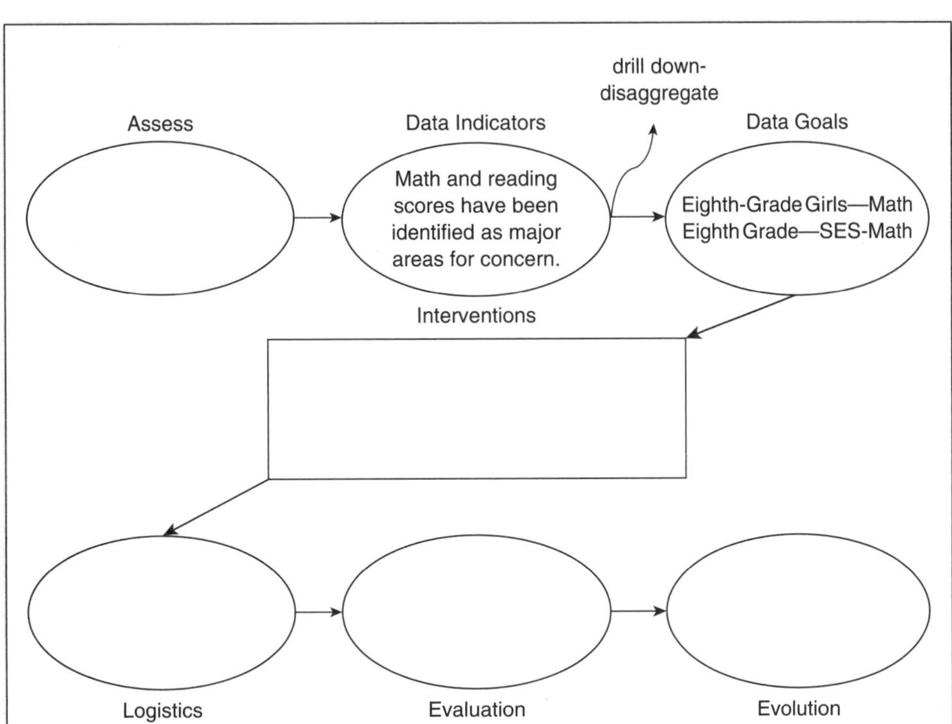

Source: Adapted from Dimmitt, Carey, & Hatch (2007).

Note: Figure 3.3 represents the logic model with an example of a data indicator and disaggregated specific data included.

Notice that we did not create specific goals for this population yet. We simply inserted the population identified as having an equity gap. Our next step is to assess what issues are currently barriers to success for these students. Notice we did not write what barriers to math achievement exist for these students. We are school counselors. It is important to remember the following: ***Data is never the problem, and data is never the solution.*** In other words, if we believe that math is the problem or make changing the math data the focus, we will not be successful. Something else is keeping the females and students receiving free or reduced-cost meals from being successful in math. We learned about the barriers to success for females through our needs assessment results. Remember, they reported the following:

- Bullying or harassment (62.0% of those polled list this as a concern)
- Rumors and gossip (50.4% of those polled list this as a concern)
- Hurting or cutting oneself (42.6% of those polled list this as a concern)
- Feeling sad or depressed a lot (42.6% of those polled list this as a concern)
- Fights or coping with stress (34.9% of those polled list this as a concern)

Certainly, any one of those issues would be enough to distract someone from academics while in school. Combined, these issues could be overwhelming. *A further step we should take is to go to the students and ask them about the issues keeping them from being successful.* We can do that through focus groups. For example, our needs assessment did not differentiate between which students are receiving free or reduced-cost lunches and which are not. As a result, we do not have any data for this population regarding what is keeping them from being successful. However, if we look at the results of the needs assessments for the entire population, we can see the following issues were identified as the five major issues overall:

- Rumors and gossip (52.5% of those polled list this as a concern)
- Bullying or harassment (47.8% of those polled list this as a concern)
- Fights (31.8% of those polled list this as a concern)
- Hurting or cutting oneself (28.7% of those polled list this as a concern)
- Feeling sad or depressed a lot (25.5% of those polled list this as a concern)

Notice that the five issues are the same, just listed in a different order. We can trust, therefore, that many of the students receiving free or reduced-cost meals probably feel similarly. However, to be sure, if it were our school, we would conduct two focus groups, one with male members receiving free or reduced-cost meals and one with females receiving free or reduced-cost meals. The members of the groups would be students scoring at a low-achieving level in math. These groups might meet twice, taking four hours of my time total the first month of school. Kaffenberger and Young (2013) call this digging process the process of "Answering a Burning Question" (p. 31). One should do whatever it takes to better understand the students' perspectives about what is going on prior to setting goals or identifying interventions.

Once the issues are clearly identified, insert them into the logic model (see Figure 3.4).

Figure 3.4 Logic Model Including Issues

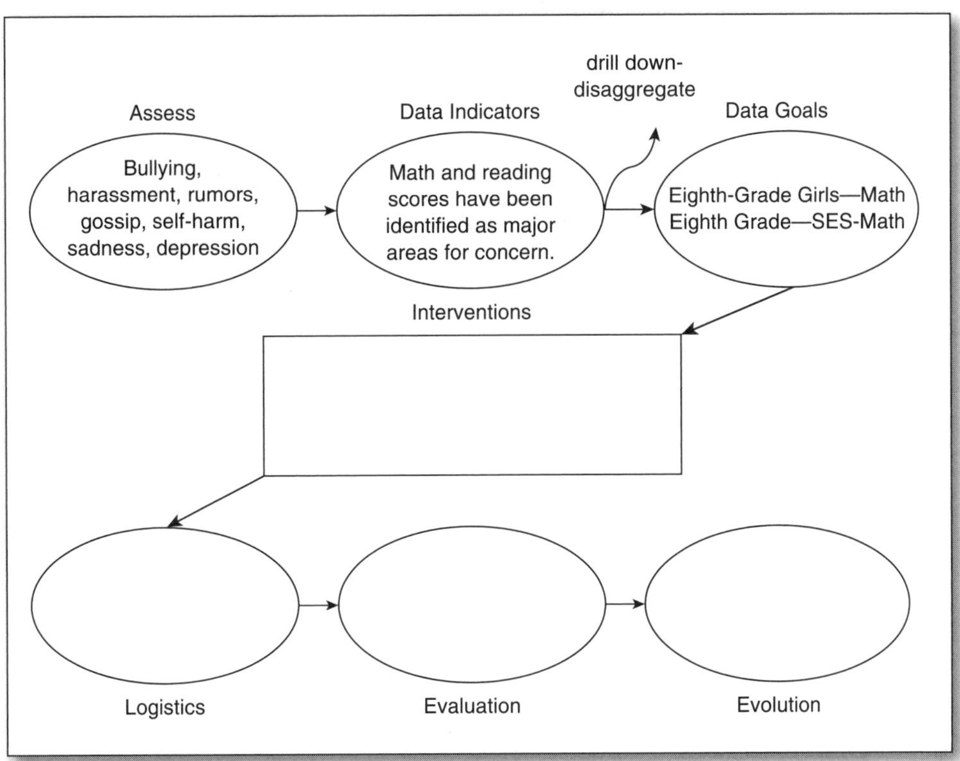

Source: Adapted from Dimmitt, Carey, & Hatch (2007).

Note: Figure 3.4 represents the logic model with an example of a data indicator, disaggregated specific data, and student issues included.

SETTING GOALS: WHO AND WHAT BUT NOT HOW—YET

We are almost ready to set rough-draft goals for our school counseling program. At this point, we can set *general goals* but not specific goals. General goals are our working, rough-draft goals that we use to explore possible interventions. Our logic model above contains two possible general, rough-draft goals. Goals must contain the specific population (the who), the baseline data (the what), the intervention (the how), and the outcome target increases (again, the what) in data if the intervention is successful. At this point, we are missing some important factors. We do not know our intervention, and therefore, we do not know how to accurately predict how much our target population should increase their math scores. Do not guess! Do not set your target goals until you know which intervention you are going to use. Then, the intervention will give you an idea of how much growth to expect. You can then insert that growth expectation into your final goal. We do not have the how, so we cannot predict growth or outcomes. However, we will evolve these rough-draft goals into more definitive goals after we determine our interventions in Chapter 5.

We have arrived at the stage in which we need to set specific, measurable outcome goals for academic growth. How do we choose the gain, either a number or a percentage, of growth we can expect for our intervention group? A variety of strategies can be applied to determine a realistic growth goal. One strategy is to obtain an expected outcome from your evidence-based intervention. If you are using an evidence-based intervention (e.g., Incredible Years, Positive Action, Second Step, Student Success Skills), the manual will have research providing previous impact of the intervention on critical data elements. For example, a school counselor can expect that if he or she uses Student Success Skills with fidelity with eighth graders that a growth of one-and-two-thirds grade level in math can be expected (Villares, Frain, Brigman, Webb, & Peluso, 2012). We can use that number to set our growth goal. If the average grade-level growth for eighth grade is four points, then the expected growth for my intervention group is almost three times that number. To keep my goal achievable, however, it may be wise to limit it to less than my highest expectation. A second strategy for determining a specific number or percentage of growth in a goal is by using the normed average growth as reported by the instrument. For example, the Measures of Academic Progress (MAP) instrument reports normed growth by grade level. (For example, from the fall of 2014 to the spring of 2015, the average growth rate for third-grade students in reading was nine points.) I can use that normed growth number to set a percentage growth that I hope my intervention group attains. If my goal is for my group to gain 10% higher scores in reading than the MAP norm, then my intervention group would need to make a ten-point gain between fall and spring assessments. A third way to set a specific data growth goal is to track historical data for your specific population. If third-grade students with individualized education plans (IEPs) have historically grown four points (notice it is less than the normed growth for that grade) between fall and spring, then perhaps a growth goal of six points for my intervention group would be realistic and achievable.

Goal One

> Eighth-grade females at our example middle school who receive our intervention will increase their math achievement scores compared to eighth-grade females who do not receive our intervention, as measured by MAP scores in fall, winter, and spring.

Goal Two

> Eighth-grade students receiving free or reduced-cost meals who receive our intervention will increase their math achievement scores 10% more than their peers who do not receive our intervention, as measured by MAP scores in fall, winter, and spring.

Notice that our two goals are only assessing the impact of students who received our intervention compared to those who did not. We want to create a natural comparison group whenever possible. It creates a much easier and clean analysis. We'll talk more about evaluation and analysis in Chapter 6. However, one rule of thumb to remember is that the more specific and clear your program goal, the easier the analysis will be later. The process of evaluation is a front-loaded process in that if you are clear with your goals, identify a specific population, are wise in your choice of intervention, and keep the setup simple, then analysis at the end will be much easier. In our experience, school counselors have found the process displayed in Figure 3.5, on the next page, to be beneficial in setting goals. Simply print out your logic model and a visual for your goal-setting sheet, and translate information from your logic model to your goal-setting sheet.

USING SMART GOALS TEMPLATE

The ASCA organizes goals into SMART goals (ASCA, 2012). Kaffenberger and Young (2013) describe SMART as an acronym for the following:

- **Specific.** Make sure the goal is based on data and target a group, instead of an entire grade or school, whenever possible.
- **Measurable.** Be sure you create a measurable goal. Which data will you use to judge whether you are effective in reaching your goal?
- **Attainable.** What outcome is attainable? We will speak to this in Chapter 5 when we discuss interventions. Examining the intervention's previous outcomes with other populations should give you an idea of what is achievable within one school year.
- **Results-oriented.** Report your results using process, perception, and outcome data.
- **Time-bound.** Be sure to articulate when the goal will be accomplished. Our two goal examples above will both be accomplished by spring of the school year.

ASCA provides templates for inserting your goal into a SMART goal template for RAMP. These templates are available on the RAMP website at

Figure 3.5 Visual for Goal Development

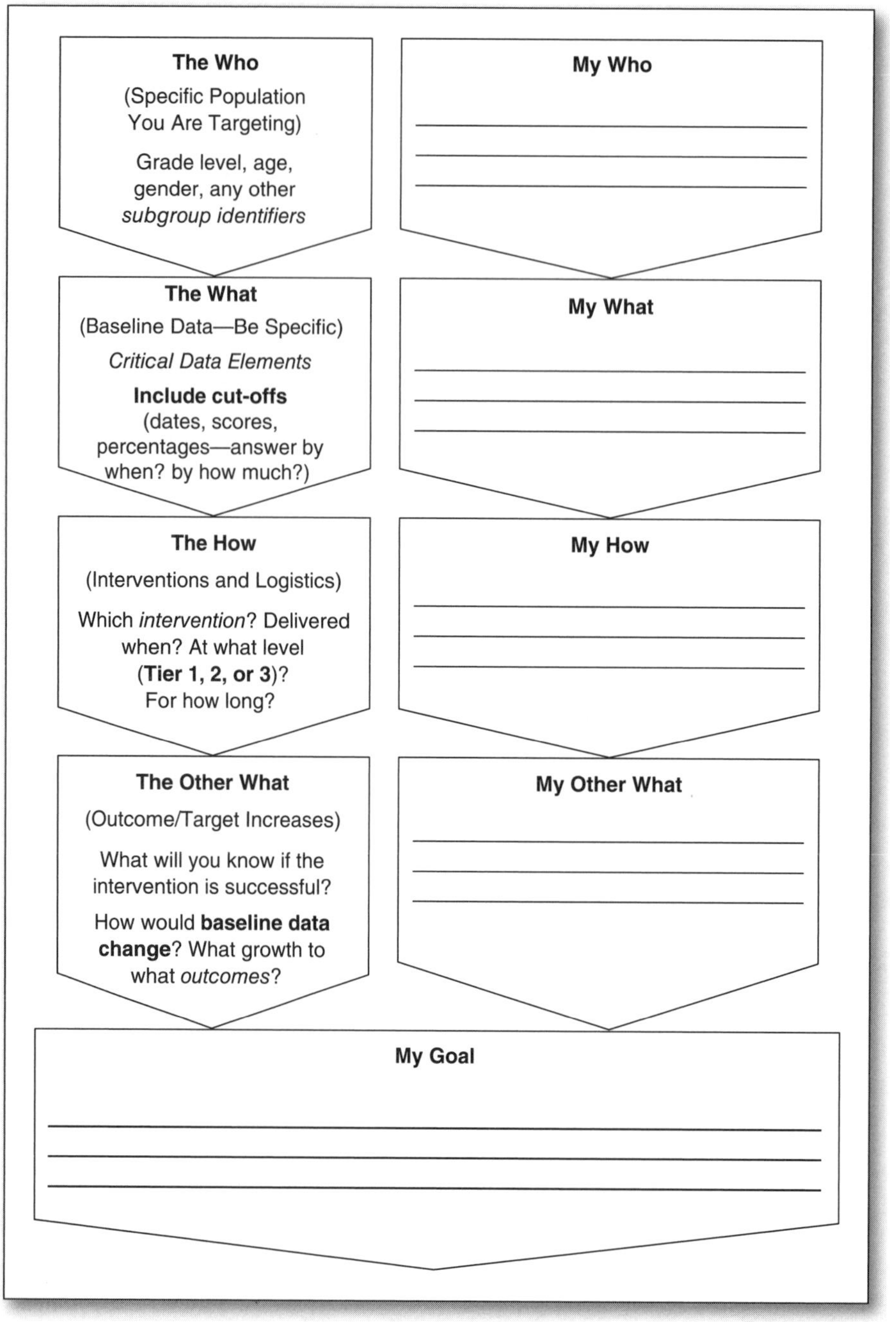

The Who

(Specific Population You Are Targeting)

Grade level, age, gender, any other *subgroup identifiers*

My Who

____

____

____

The What

(Baseline Data—Be Specific)

Critical Data Elements

Include cut-offs (dates, scores, percentages—answer by when? by how much?)

My What

____

____

____

The How

(Interventions and Logistics)

Which *intervention*? Delivered when? At what level (**Tier 1, 2, or 3**)? For how long?

My How

____

____

____

The Other What

(Outcome/Target Increases)

What will you know if the intervention is successful?

How would **baseline data change**? What growth to what *outcomes*?

My Other What

____

____

____

My Goal

____

____

____

Note: Figure 3.5 represents a step-by-step guide for goal setting.

https://www.schoolcounselor.org/school-counselors-members/asca-national-model/asca-national-model-templates.

FULFILLING COMPONENTS OF RAMP

Setting SMART goals directly addresses Item 3 of the RAMP application: school counseling program goals. The RAMP application (https://www.schoolcounselor.org/school-counselors-members/ramp/application-process) states, "The school counseling program goals give focus to the school counseling program. They define how the vision and mission are accomplished and guide the development of curriculum, small-group and closing-the-gap action plans." Further, the goals must focus on achievement, attendance, or behavior or school safety issues. Notice that each of the issues required as points of focus measure behavior change in students. The goals developed through the data-driven decision-making process match the required focus of RAMP goals. In fact, the RAMP application requires that the program goals are "based on school data . . . address academic, career, and/or social/emotional development . . . (and) are SMART."

Also, remember that the narratives related to how each RAMP component was developed need to be rich and include "how goals were developed, how they address student learning and/or student inequalities, and how they are founded in data" (https://www.schoolcounselor.org/asca/media/asca/RAMP/Rubric.pdf). Again, the process detailed above meets those qualifications. It is important to examine what is needed to earn a score of five points for each RAMP criteria. To achieve a full five-point score for the school counseling goals, it is important to ensure that each of the requirements listed above are met. Further, the narrative needs to provide a detailed description of the process by which the goals were developed, how the data was used, how these populations were chosen, how the interventions were chosen, how the outcome goals were identified, and how it is all founded in data.

4 Beliefs, Mission, and Vision

A Checklist for Building Beliefs, Mission, and Vision	
Completed?	**Processes (including any necessary materials)**
❒	Download examples of others schools' beliefs, missions, and visions.
❒	Build a belief statement. Check to ensure the language reflects why you became a school counselor.
❒	Collect your state department of education's mission statement, your school district's mission statement, and your school's mission statement.
❒	Collect your state department of education's vision statement, your school district's vision statement, and your school's vision statement.
❒	Build the school counseling program's mission statement.
❒	Build the school counseling program's vision statement.
❒	Practice scoring your mission and vision statements using the RAMP rubric.

It may be that the natural progression from our rough-draft goals would be to move directly to exploring our interventions. However, creating the foundation for our school counseling program can provide a solid core that helps define the direction we choose for our interventions. This chapter will provide easy templates and a process for creating the beliefs, mission, and vision of a school counseling program. Too often, these foundational core tenets of our programs are given lip service and never revisited. Many states, districts, and schools create mission statements that are never used to drive the focus and direction of the momentum of the organization. When created properly these three components can provide an infrastructure upon which programs and interventions can be built while also maintaining a clear focus to keep the program from being spread too thin, rendering it ineffective. In the visual of Figure 4.1, the evidence-based school counseling process, the beliefs, mission, and vision are at the core of the circle. This chapter will build from the beliefs to the mission and conclude with the vision of the school counseling program.

Figure 4.1 Process for Building Evidence-Based School Counseling Program

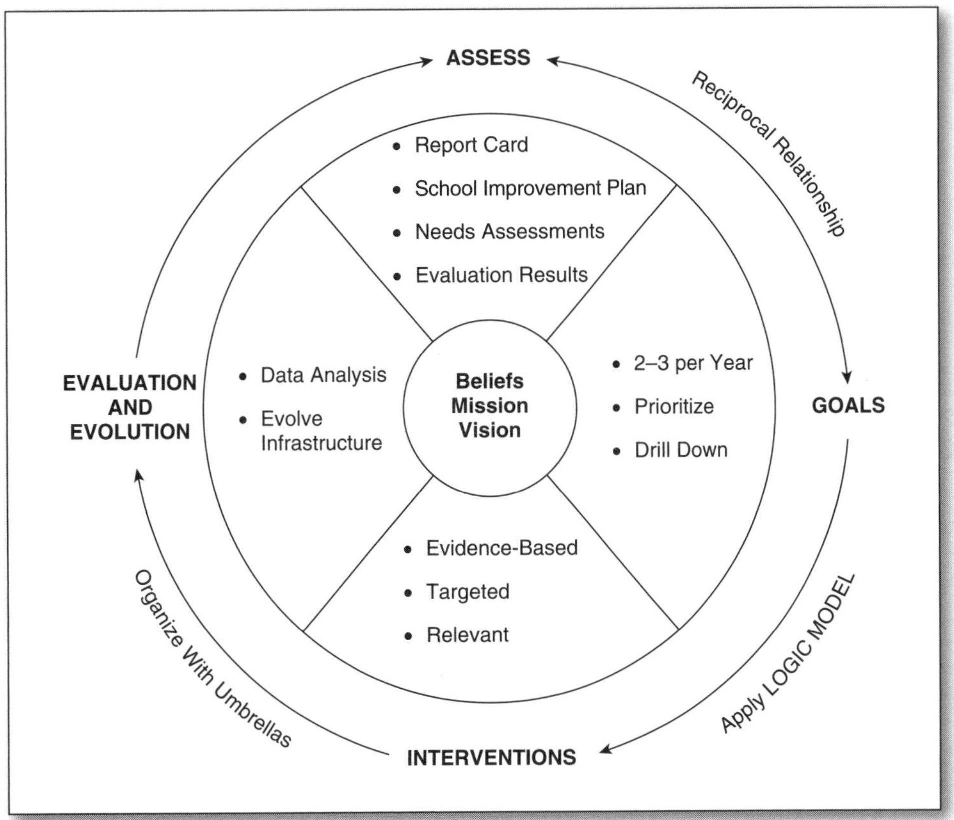

Note: The arrows indicate the reciprocal relationship of various aspects of the process.

BELIEFS

One of the mistakes that school counselors often make is completing the beliefs, mission, and vision simply to fulfill RAMP requirements. It is easy to understand how this occurs, as educational entities often create beliefs that are never revisited or used to focus the mission of the organization. However, in business models, this is not the case. The best companies are run with an eye on the belief systems. For example, William Hewlett and David Packard founded Hewlett-Packard Co. in a garage in 1938 and created a management system of respect and shared governance later branded "The HP Way." As long as those two were in charge, the HP Way, their belief system, focused the manner in which the company functioned. The beliefs are the foundation upon which the infrastructure is built.

Use the creation of the beliefs to share what called you to pursue school counseling as your profession. These can change depending upon the school counselor. This is where you are encouraged to share your passion, drive, and motivation for being in this profession. Focus your program through the creation of your beliefs about students, your beliefs about school counselors, and your beliefs about the school counseling program. This is the heart of your school counseling program. It should be student focused, and your personality should shine through. Some commonalities exist across various schools' belief systems, and those universal beliefs of our profession will be shared below. However, some of the beliefs should be specific to you and your program. Examples of unique beliefs will also be highlighted.

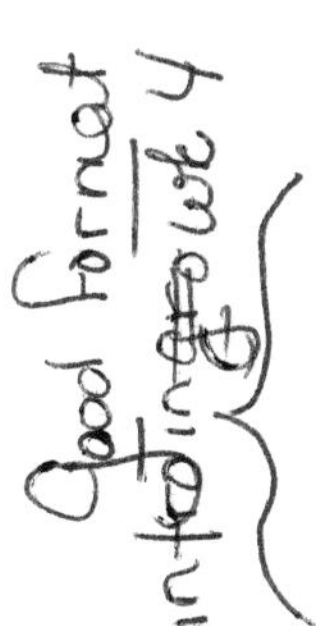

To create a strong belief statement, the school counselors at Campbell County Middle School (CCMS) in Alexandria, Kentucky, found organizing the beliefs in the following manner helped their conceptualization and application. They organized their beliefs by starting the sentences with (a) "All students . . . (have something or do something)" and then transitioned to (b) "School counselors . . . (have something or do something)" and then transitioned to (c) "The school counseling program . . . (has something or does something)." Take the following example:

The School Counselors at Campbell County Middle School believe:

- *All students* have significance and worth.
- All students—regardless of ability, age, gender, ethnicity, or sexual orientation—shall have equal access to all services (academic, career, and social/emotional) provided by the counseling program and the school.
- All students have strengths that can be applied to achieve their goals.
- All students learn best when positive relationships are present and fostered by all educational stakeholders.
- *School counselors* must be advocates for every student.

- School counselors are leaders and change agents in school culture and academic achievement.
- School counselors develop positive relationships and recognize each student's special talents to help them achieve goals.
- *The school counseling program* collaborates with educational stakeholders to increase equity and access to opportunity.
- The school counseling program serves a central role in meeting students' developmental needs through interventions in academic, career, and social/emotional domains.
- The school counseling program focuses on student learning and utilizes a data-driven comprehensive school counseling program to meet the needs of every student.
- The comprehensive school counseling program is tailored to meet students' developmental needs as identified through needs assessments, delivered using evidence-based programs, and evolved through data analysis of outcomes.
- The school counseling program utilizes the American School Counselor Association ethical standards.

You may not agree with all the beliefs contained in the Campbell County Middle School counseling program's belief statements above. Or you may think that some foundational beliefs need to be added. Again, your passion areas should exude from your belief statement. For example, CCMS's school counselors wanted to emphasize the role that positive relationships between students and everyone at the school and in the community have on student success. So they created this specific belief statement addressing that issue: *All students learn best when positive relationships are present and fostered by all educational stakeholders.* Spend time developing beliefs that are unique to your program, your school population, and you personally, as a professional school counselor.

Which belief statements are foundational components of our profession? It is the authors' suggestion that belief statements regarding equity, access, and ethical practice should be contained in every school counseling program's belief statement. Thus, the following beliefs may be considered appropriate for every school:

- All students—regardless of ability, age, gender, ethnicity, or sexual orientation—shall have equal access to all services (academic, career, and social/emotional) provided by the counseling program and the school.
- School counselors must be advocates for every student.
- The school counseling program collaborates with educational stakeholders to increase equity and access to opportunity.
- The school counseling program utilizes the American School Counselor Association's ethical standards.

If your program is focused on developing an evidence-based, data-driven comprehensive school counseling program, the following beliefs may be relevant to your program:

- The school counseling program focuses on student learning and utilizes a data-driven comprehensive school counseling program to meet the needs of every student.
- The comprehensive school counseling program is tailored to meet students' developmental needs as identified through needs assessments, delivered using evidence-based programs, and evolved through data analysis of outcomes.

The outline in Figure 4.2 has been created to help you create beliefs relevant to your school. We have added five belief statements for each

Figure 4.2 Belief Statement Worksheet

The school counselors at ______________________________ School believe

- All students have significance and worth.
- All students—regardless of ability, age, gender, ethnicity, or sexual orientation—shall have equal access to all services (academic, career, and social/emotional) provided by the counseling program and the school.
- All students ____

  ____

  ____

  ____
- All students ____

  ____

  ____

  ____
- All students ____

  ____

  ____

  ____
- School counselors must be advocates for every student.

- School counselors ____
____
____
____

- School counselors ____
____
____
____

- School counselors ____
____
____
____

- School counselors ____
____
____
____

- The school counseling program collaborates with educational stakeholders to increase equity and access to opportunity.

- The school counseling program ____
____
____
____

- The school counseling program focuses on student learning and utilizes a data-driven comprehensive school counseling program to meet the needs of every student.
- The comprehensive school counseling program is tailored to meet students' developmental needs as identified through needs assessments, delivered using evidence-based programs, and evolved through data analysis of outcomes.
- The school counseling program utilizes the American School Counselor Association's ethical standards.

category: (a) all students, (b) school counselors, and (c) the school counseling program. This is only for your convenience as you create the belief statement for your school. You may have additional or fewer statements in each category. Additional examples of other schools' belief statements are included in Appendix A and in the online resource center (http://www.corwin.com/ZyromskiEvidenceBased).

MISSION

Although the RAMP rubric (ASCA, 2014) does not detail requirements for what is contained within the belief statement, only that it be included in the vision section of your submission, specific requirements for the mission statement are detailed within the RAMP rubric.

The school counseling mission statement:

1. Aligns with the school's mission statement and may show linkages to district and state department of education mission statements
2. Is written with students as the primary focus
3. Advocates for equity, access and success of every student
4. Indicates the long-range results desired for all students. (ASCA, 2014, p. 3)

Using the foundation and focus created by our belief statement and fulfilling the four components listed by RAMP, creating a dynamic mission statement can be a structured, straightforward process.

First, obtain your state's educational mission statement. Second, obtain your school district's educational mission statement. And finally, obtain your school's educational mission statement. (Use Figure 4.3 to help organize these statements.) You can obtain these mission statements by using the Google search engine (e.g., Kentucky Department of Education Mission).

Once you have obtained all three levels of mission statements, begin incorporating key words from those mission statements into the mission statement of your school counseling program. Remember to (a) keep students as the primary focus, (b) advocate for equity, access, and success for every student, (c) personalize it to your population, your unique environment in the school and surrounding community, and the developmental level of your students, and (d) indicate long-term outcomes for your students. An example mission statement has been provided to you in Figure 4.4 on page 48. Notice how the example incorporates the keys words and pieces mentioned above.

Figure 4.3 Obtaining Mission Statements

State's Educational Mission Statement

____

____

____

____

School District's Educational Mission Statement

____

____

____

____

School's Educational Mission Statement

____

____

____

____

Notice in Figure 4.4, which can also be found on the school counseling program website (http://www.tichenormiddleschool.com/?page_id=1457), that the focus on individual needs of students posited by the district's mission statement is repeated within the school counseling program's mission statement—"embrace and attend to the individual needs of students regardless of the obstacles." The focus of the middle school's mission statement is serving all students and using an accountability-based education. The school counseling program again emphasizes similar foci without using the same language. When the school counseling program speaks to "empirically supported, data-driven comprehensive school counseling programming," it refers to programming that results in accountability for the school counseling program. The evidence-based, data-driven approach also helps school counselors assess the progress and growth of students, another important piece of accountability. Additional examples of other schools' mission statements are included in Appendix B and in the online resource center (http://www.corwin.com/ZyromskiEvidenceBased).

Figure 4.4 Example Mission Statement

State of Kentucky Educational Mission Statement

The Kentucky Department of Education's mission is to prepare all Kentucky students for next-generation learning, work and citizenship by engaging schools, districts, families, and communities through excellent leadership, service, and support.

Erlanger-Elsmere Independent School District's Mission Statement

It is the mission of the Erlanger-Elsmere Schools to embrace and attend to the individual needs of our students, regardless of the obstacles.

Tichenor Middle School's Mission Statement

Tichenor Middle School shall provide a quality, accountability-based education in academics, arts, and athletics; producing responsible citizens by equipping all students with global skills, knowledge, understanding, and dispositions required for the 21st Century College to Career.

Tichenor Middle School Counseling Program Mission Statement

Tichenor Middle School Counseling Program removes barriers to success for all students through empirically supported, data-driven comprehensive school counseling programming. At Tichenor Middle School, all stakeholders, such as teachers, administrators, parents/guardians, families, caretakers, youth service center, and a caring community, embrace and attend to the individual needs of students regardless of the obstacles in the domains of academic, career, and personal/social to emphasize **meaningful learning**. The Tichenor Middle School Counseling Program increases equity through diverse programming, organized through response to intervention to meet the needs of all students.

It may be useful to think about the interrelationship between the beliefs, mission, and vision in the following way: We articulate who we are and our values that define our school counseling program in our belief statement. We operationalize those beliefs—we put those values and priorities into action—in our mission statement. Finally, if we are successful in our mission, we will know because we will have accomplished our vision for the school counseling program. Hence, the vision is how we will know we have accomplished the mission of the program.

VISION

The RAMP rubric describes the vision as "what school counselors want to see in the future for the school community related to student achievement and other outcomes." In the evidence-based school counseling process, we need to be able to assess if we have accomplished the vision of the school counseling program. Hence, the organization of an evidence-based vision statement might differ slightly from the components required for a top score for RAMP. As a result, we will describe how to create a vision that is easily assessed to ensure you can continue to evolve your mission, programming, and interventions. The difference between the two is that an evidence-based vision statement focuses on the ability of the school counselor to assess when that vision has been achieved. RAMP requires that the vision "outlines a rich and textual picture of what success looks and feels like" and "is bold and inspiring." In our minds, although these two facets are valuable, practical evaluation is a higher priority. The practical vision statement can be easily evolved to one that is bold and inspiring, satisfying both objectives.

The first step in building a vision statement is similar to the first step of building a mission statement. Collect the vision statement of your state's educational department. Second, obtain your school district's educational vision statement. And finally, obtain your school's educational vision statement (use Figure 4.5 to help organize these statements). You can obtain these

Figure 4.5 Obtaining Vision Statements

State's Educational Vision Statement

____

____

____

____

School District's Educational Vision Statement

____

____

____

____

School's Educational Vision Statement

____

____

____

____

vision statements by using the Google search engine (e.g., Kentucky Department of Education Vision). However, unlike mission statements, vision statements are not always created and posted by educational organizations. Your state may not have a vision statement, your school district may not have a vision statement, and your school may not have a vision statement. Just insert an N/A when that occurs and move on to the next level.

We are going to use Tichenor Middle School's counseling program as our model for building the vision statement. Additional examples of other schools' vision statements are contained in the online resource center (http://www.corwin.com/ZyromskiEvidenceBased). Tichenor Middle School's vision statement is contained in Figure 4.6, Example Vision Statement.

Figure 4.6 Example Vision Statement

State of Kentucky Educational Vision Statement

The vision of the Kentucky Board of Education is to ensure that all students reach proficiency and graduate from high school ready for college and careers.

Erlanger-Elsmere Independent School District's Vision Statement

The Erlanger-Elsmere Schools will provide essential opportunities for all students to reach their greatest potential.

Tichenor Middle School's Vision Statement

Tichenor Middle School will empower dreamers to achieve excellence in all facets of life.

Tichenor Middle School's Counseling Program Vision Statement

Tichenor Middle School's Counseling Program will realize success when students:

- Leave middle school with a vision for their life that includes clear expectations for themselves, exhibiting a personal compass built from their values, interests, and passions, and having set clear and achievable steps for obtaining their goals.
- Successfully transition to high school and beyond, using college and career readiness skills to navigate and overcome barriers to positively contribute to society.
- Exhibit self-awareness of their strengths and weaknesses and use that knowledge to propel them towards achieving identified goals.
- Are involved in positive connections and mentorship relationships with adults, are able to recognize and seek help when needed, and are positive role models and mentors for others.
- Are active partners with the school counseling program, community stakeholders, families, and school resources.
- Continue to seek learning opportunities, enhance society with their talents, and make a positive difference in their families and communities.

Notice that the vision statement is organized in such a way that the school counselors can assess whether each piece of the vision is accomplished. Hopefully, the vision is simply organized just how it would look if the mission and goals of the school counseling program were accomplished. If the school counseling program's mission was accomplished, how would we know? What knowledge, dispositions, or skills would students exhibit? If the goals of the school counseling program were achieved, how would we know? What knowledge, dispositions, or skills would students exhibit?

For example, in Tichenor Middle School's counseling program vision statement, school counselors can assess whether or not students are able to set clear and achievable steps for obtaining their goals. This assessment can occur during college and career programming. School counselors can collaborate with the high school counselors to track students' success in the transition from middle to high school. An instrument could be used to assess whether or not students exhibit self-awareness of their strengths and weaknesses. As you continue reading down through the various points describing the vision of the school counseling program, you may notice that it is possible to assess, in some way, if the students accomplish these outcomes. Each of the points is evaluative.

However, in this format, the vision statement will not earn a five-point score (out of a possible five points) during the RAMP evaluation process. Although the vision is reflected in the mission and goals of the school counseling program—organized in language that makes it possible to assess whether they were achieved—the vision is not "bold and inspiring." It is important that when the reviewers read your vision statement, they feel inspired. Therefore, once you have created the various bullet points that describe the mission and goals of the school counseling program to be achieved and the knowledge, dispositions, and skills students would exhibit if they were achieved, use that content to create a paragraph that is inspiring.

For example, the contents of the bullet points were incorporated into a paragraph that will please evaluators in Figure 4.7 on the next page.

As school counselors create strong, clear, and concise belief statements, mission statements, and vision statements, they not only provide a focus and clear direction to the school counseling program, but they also communicate the values, priorities, and outcomes of their program to all stakeholders. Students, parents, administrators, and teachers all require training in what school counselors do, how priorities of the program are identified, and how school counselors are different from teachers or other educators in the school. One of the main tasks of any school counseling program is to determine how to provide services to all students while prioritizing interventions for students suffering from equity gaps and a lack of access to opportunity. Clearly distributing and posting the school counseling beliefs, mission, and vision articulates how the school counseling program serves students and the school.

Figure 4.7 Example Vision Statement: Paragraph Added

State of Kentucky Educational Vision Statement

The vision of the Kentucky Board of Education is to ensure that all students reach proficiency and graduate from high school ready for college and careers.

Erlanger-Elsmere Independent School District's Vision Statement

The Erlanger-Elsmere Schools will provide essential opportunities for all students to reach their greatest potential.

Tichenor Middle School's Vision Statement

Tichenor Middle School will empower dreamers to achieve excellence in all facets of life.

Tichenor Middle School's Counseling Program Vision Statement

The vision of the Tichenor Middle School Counseling Program is for students to apply their personal compass to achieve their personal goals and positively contribute to their families and society as a whole. Students will leave Tichenor Middle School with a vision for their lives and will successfully transition to high school and then to post-secondary college and/or career options. As a result of school counseling interventions, students will increase their self-awareness, apply college-and-career readiness skills, and apply their strengths to overcome barriers to success. Students will become life-long learners and enhance society with their talents.

Tichenor Middle School's Counseling Program will realize success when students:

- Leave middle school with a vision for their life that includes clear expectations for themselves, exhibiting a personal compass built from their values, interests, and passions, and having set clear and achievable steps for obtaining their goals.
- Successfully transition to high school and beyond, using college and career readiness skills to navigate and overcome barriers to positively contribute to society.
- Exhibit self-awareness of their strengths and weaknesses and use that knowledge to propel them towards achieving identified goals.
- Are involved in positive connections and mentorship relationships with adults, are able to recognize and seek help when needed, and are positive role models and mentors for others.
- Are active partners with the school counseling program, community stakeholders, families, and school resources.
- Continue to seek learning opportunities, enhance society with their talents, and make a positive difference in their families and communities.

FULFILLING COMPONENTS OF RAMP

The vision statement is the first component of the RAMP application. Within the vision statement submission, the applicant is required to include a list of the school counseling program beliefs. The mission statement is the second component of the RAMP application. The beliefs, mission, and vision are primary documents required for the RAMP application. Other components of the RAMP application require the applicant to connect that component back to the beliefs, mission, and vision of the program. For example, the goal-setting component (Component Three) requires the applicant to detail how the school counseling program goals align with the mission and vision of the school counseling program.

The exact RAMP criteria for the mission statement are as follows:

The school counseling mission statement:

1. Aligns with the school's mission statement and may show linkages to district and state department of education mission statements
2. Is written with students as the primary focus
3. Advocates for equity, access, and success of every student
4. Indicates the long-range results desired for all students. (ASCA, 2014, p. 3)

The exact RAMP criteria for the vision statement are as follows:

The school counseling vision statement:

1. Describes a future world where the school counseling goals and strategies are being successfully achieved
2. Outlines a rich and textual picture of what success looks and feels like
3. Is bold and inspiring
4. States the best possible student outcomes that are five to 15 years away
5. Is believable and achievable

Include:

- A list of the school counseling program's beliefs.
- A copy of the school and district vision statements (if available).

Note: If your school/district does not have a vision statement, please indicate in the narrative. (ASCA, 2014, p. 1)

5 Interventions

A Checklist for Identifying and Selecting Intentional, Evidence-Based Interventions	
Completed?	**Processes (including any necessary materials)**
❒	Target key topics or areas and compare them to goals (*check for alignment*).
❒	Determine data to be collected before, during, and after the intervention (*be intentional*).
❒	Refer to the list of SC evidence-based interventions (provided), cross-reference it with the key areas identified, consult research supporting intervention, and gain approval to implement (*be targeted*).
❒	Fulfill program training requirements, purchase a manual or other supplemental materials, and deliver the program in the manner it was designed (*tend to fidelity*).

PURPOSE OF INTENTIONAL INTERVENTIONS

This book is about intentional professional practice—purposefully choosing how to operate in your role as a school counselor to be a catalyst for positive systemic change for your students. Let's go back and once again refer to the visual process for creating an evidence-based school counseling program (see Figure 5.1 on page 56). Notice that we are now at the bottom of our logic model where our task is to select evidence-based interventions that are both relevant and targeted (no random acts of selection here). Intentionally selecting interventions is not a willy-nilly process. Rather, it's a process that requires

STEP-BY-STEP GUIDE FOR SELECTING EVIDENCE-BASED INTERVENTIONS

1. Based on the information you have collected from your needs assessments, target key topics or areas where students are lacking skills that require school counseling interventions.
2. Compare these key topics or areas for alignment with the goals you have identified, which are articulated in your school counseling program goals from Chapter 3 (*check for alignment*).
3. Determine what types of data (process, perception, or results/outcome) will be collected before, during, and after the intervention (*be intentional*). Examine the population of need identified in your goal, and select what outcome(s) you want to effect. (*What outcomes are important to you, your students, and your stakeholders?*) Layer your outcome data, when possible, using various sources (perception or results).
4. Refer to the list of school counseling evidence-based interventions provided and cross-reference it with the key areas you identified; you may also refer to the online resource center (http://www.corwin.com/ZyromskiEvidenceBased) for additional programs. This does not mean that you have to provide an evidence-based intervention for every grade or all students in the school at this point. . . . Remember to start small and build! Go through the process described in the previous chapters to identify your target population and match the intervention to their (the students') identified needs (*be targeted*).
5. Consult the professional literature and research supporting your chosen interventions. Review and understand the information regarding "expected outcomes." This language can assist you in explaining the need for this program to your administrators, teachers, and parents (*be able to "sell" this program*).
6. Gain approval from administrators and teachers regarding time allotted in your schedule to provide this intervention to students. Consider piloting the intervention in collaboration with one or two teachers that you consider allies in the school. Just be sure that you are hitting the population that expressed the needs matched by your intervention.
7. Review any program requirements including training and/or purchasing a manual or other supplemental materials. Deliver the

(Continued)

(Continued)

program in the manner it was designed. Pay specific attention to fidelity practices (covered in this chapter). If you are unable to deliver the program or intervention according to the design, record these changes and/or modifications. However, make note that these variations are likely to impact your outcomes (*tend to fidelity*).

careful review of the current school counseling curriculum or programs available and checking them for alignment with the present needs of our students (as reflected in our needs assessments and resulting school goals).

Dimmitt, Carey, and Hatch (2007) define evidence-based practice as the intentional planning and implementation of programs and interventions that can be linked to proximal and distal outcomes. We will review various

Figure 5.1 Process for Building Evidence-Based School Counseling Program

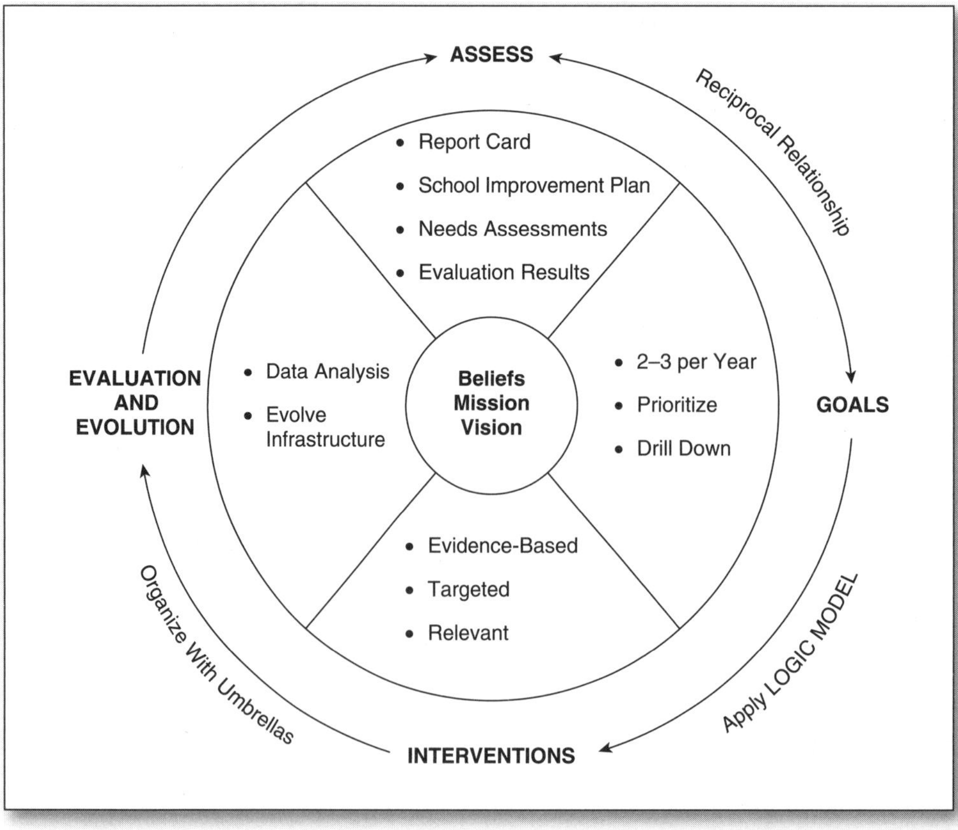

Note: The arrows indicate the reciprocal relationship of various aspects of the process.

sources of data in this chapter and provide recommendations for which types have the most influence for key stakeholders. Ideally, the connection should be made to both types of data (we refer to this as "layering your data"), but let's not bite off more than we can chew for now. Remember, keep it simple at first, and over time, build on your successes.

WHY EVIDENCE-BASED INTERVENTIONS?

We will now begin to walk through the steps for choosing evidence-based interventions. As outlined above, your **first step** in selecting appropriate interventions is to make a list of the key areas or topics that require school counseling services (refer to "Tips and Tricks"). This list will be derived from the results of your needs assessments (refer to Chapters 2 and 3). **Second**, revisit what types of outcome data you plan to collect (process, perception, or results). As previously mentioned, there are various types of data. However, in order to maximize your program's impact (and communicate changes that administrators and key stakeholders care most about), we need to collect and analyze data that will be the most powerful communicators of the achievement or behavior change of students. When we consider what data types to collect, we want to ask ourselves, *How are students different as a result of our efforts?* and, *What school counseling interventions are we implementing that can be directly tied to improved student achievement and behavior?* Though process and perception data provide some important information, the most powerful source (particularly for administrators) is results-based or outcome data. Consider, as well, having multiple data collection points (before, during, and after the intervention). Longitudinal data—results that show the lasting impact of school counseling interventions—are particularly valuable. You might also choose to "layer your data" by collecting data from various sources over time. We highly recommend this practice as your results on different measures may vary. Thus, investigating the problem in multiple ways can help stack the deck in your favor.

Let's take a moment here to review possible sources of data. Recall that descriptive data about your school counseling program (who, what, where, when, and why) are not as useful as student perception data and results data. Examples of perception data reflected in student outcomes include changes in students' skills, abilities, and perceptions. Ideally, improvements reflected in student perception data (information that may seem arbitrary or inconsequential to school leaders) eventually get reflected in results data. (This is what your administrators and district leaders are most interested in.) This school-level data, or results data as we are referring to it here, may include things like grade point averages, standardized test scores, school grades, AP course completions and scores, disciplinary referrals, suspension and expulsion rates, graduation rates, post-secondary attendance rates, and drop-out rates. As a reminder, though student perception data is useful, honing in on results data is what will get your leaders to view you and your interventions as key to your school's success. The possible perception data and results data that align with various evidence-based interventions we recommend are listed in Table 5.1.

EVIDENCE-BASED INTERVENTIONS MATRIX

Create a matrix. Choose from these, and if you don't find one that hits your issues, go to the resources listed in Table 5.2 (page 66).

In your **third step,** we get into the meat of this chapter, reviewing possible evidence-based school counseling interventions, those that meet the areas of concern we listed in **Step 1**. Begin by selecting from the list of programs we have provided, as these have been scrutinized by the Center for School Counseling Outcome Research and Evaluation, the What Works Clearinghouse, and documented outcome studies. Other programs and interventions can be accessed using the links provided in this chapter and by referring to the online resource center (http://www.corwin.com/ZyromskiEvidenceBased).

Interventions can be viewed in terms of schoolwide interventions (accessible to all students) and targeted interventions (which address specific needs for selected grade levels, groups, or individuals). Table 5.1 provides a quick reference of some evidence-based school counseling interventions. (This list is in no way exhaustive.) In addition to the problem areas these programs target, Table 5.1 also includes the ways in which the program has been assessed and evidenced outcomes that have resulted from proper implementation of these interventions. Finally, Table 5.1 lists sources to be consulted should you be interested in learning more about or ordering these programs. Additional programs can be found by consulting the resources listed in Table 5.2.

Next, in **Step 4**, you should read, review, and understand the research documenting your selected program's effectiveness. What are the *expected outcomes* that have been linked to this intervention? Though this is often explained in the studies documented in professional journals as an *effect size*, what this term really describes is the practical significance of the intervention, or what one can realistically expect to see in terms of outcomes if the program is implemented correctly. Educating yourself about the program's theoretical and research base will help you in gaining support from administrators, teachers, parents, and, most importantly, your students. A critical piece of being able to effectively implement a program is having the buy-in of those key stakeholders. If they don't see the value,

(Text continued on page 66)

Table 5.1 List of Evidence-Based Interventions and Corresponding Data Elements

Program/Curriculum (method of implementation)	Grade Level	Purpose/ Targeted Area of Improvement	Possible Perception and Results Data Sources	Evidenced Outcomes	Source
Bridges' Proactive School Curriculum—Transitions (CG)	6–12	College and career readiness skills Academic achievement	Enrollment in AP courses Number of college applications Number of financial aid applications ACT, SAT, or AP exam scores Graduation and dropout rates Post-secondary attendance rates Successful employment outcomes	Work-related behaviors (absences, tardiness, and performance evaluations) Job acquisition and job retention rates	http://www.xap.com/Products-Services/Transitions/Counselors/Highlights-Features.asp
Bully Busters (SG)	K–5	School-based aggression and bullying behaviors Social skills Coping skills	Teacher reports Student self-reports Survey information (related to increased awareness, knowledge, and skills) Behavior incident reports Bullying reports Disciplinary referrals	Teacher perceptions Student perceptions related to bullying Peer aggression School or classroom climates	https://www.researchpress.com/books/455/bully-busters Research support: Newman-Carlson and Horne (2004)

(Continued)

Table 5.1 (Continued)

Program/Curriculum (method of implementation)	Grade Level	Purpose/ Targeted Area of Improvement	Possible Perception and Results Data Sources	Evidenced Outcomes	Source
Character Counts (CG)	preK–12	Six Pillars of Character: trustworthiness, respect, responsibility, caring, citizenship, and fairness	Teacher reports Student self-reports Survey information (related to increased awareness, knowledge, and skills) Behavior referrals Incident reports Test scores Graduation rates	Reduction in suspensions and expulsions Increased parent, teacher, and student satisfaction with school Improved behavior and attitudes Improved standardized test scores Improved graduation rates	https://charactercounts.org/research/summary.html
Coping Cat (IC)	K–12	Anxiety-related behaviors and symptoms	Teacher reports Student self-reports Survey information (related to increased awareness, knowledge, and skills) Behavioral observations Attendance rates	Reductions in anxiety and fear Improved ability to cope Reductions in negative thoughts and reduced depressive symptoms	http://www.workbookpublishing.com/product_info.php?products_id=30
The Incredible Years	preK–2	Promote emotional, social, and academic competence	Teacher and parent reports Student self-reports Survey information (related to increased awareness, knowledge, and skills)	Increased school readiness Emotional regulation and social competence Improved parenting interactions and relationships	http://incredibleyears.com/research-library/key-research/

Program/Curriculum (method of implementation)	Grade Level	Purpose/ Targeted Area of Improvement	Possible Perception and Results Data Sources	Evidenced Outcomes	Source
		Prevent, reduce, and treat behavioral and emotional problems (decrease risk factors and increase protective factors)	Behavioral observations Attendance rates Discipline referrals School grades Achievement indicators Promotion and retention rates	Improved teaching and relationships with students and parents Reduced dropout rates Increased academic achievement Reduced youth conduct disorders and criminal activity Reduced drug and alcohol problems	
Olweus Bullying Prevention Program (OBPP) (CG)	K–12	Bullying, aggression School safety Classroom and school climate Academic performance	Teacher reports Student self-reports Survey information (related to increased awareness, knowledge, and skills) Standardized test scores and school grades Attendance rates Discipline referrals and bullying reports	Reduced student reports of bullying Reduced antisocial behaviors Improved classroom climate Positive social relationships and positive attitudes toward school Significant increase in standardized test scores in English, math, science, and history	http://www .violenceprevention works.org/public/ olweus_research .page

(Continued)

Table 5.1 (Continued)

Program/Curriculum (method of implementation)	Grade Level	Purpose/ Targeted Area of Improvement	Possible Perception and Results Data Sources	Evidenced Outcomes	Source
Peacebuilders Intervention (CG)	preK–12	Resilience and social competence Bullying, aggression, and school climate	Teacher reports Student self-reports Survey information (related to increased awareness, knowledge, and skills) Behavior referrals and bullying incidents	Reductions in future delinquent, violent, and antisocial behavior Improved social competence Improved school climate Increased prosocial skills and peace-building behaviors	https://www.peacebuilders.com/media/pdfs/research/CounselingOutcomeResearch.pdf https://www.peacebuilders.com/whatWeDo/research.php
Positive Action (CG)	K–12	Student achievement and behavior Can be applied to a host of different problem areas (https://www.positiveaction.net/overview/applications)	Teacher and parent reports Student self-reports Survey information (related to increased awareness, knowledge, and skills) Behavior referrals and bullying incidents Suspension rates Absentee rates Standardized test scores	Effects of the program range from increased academic achievement to dramatic reductions in problem behaviors. These results have been replicated in diverse settings and feature the most rigorous efficacy study designs available.	https://www.positiveaction.net/research/outcomes/all-outcomes

Program/Curriculum (method of implementation)	Grade Level	Purpose/ Targeted Area of Improvement	Possible Perception and Results Data Sources	Evidenced Outcomes	Source
Ready to Learn (CG)	preK–1	Reading comprehension Listening comprehension Attending skills Student achievement Behavior	Teacher and parent reports Student self-reports Survey information (related to increased awareness, knowledge, and skills) Standardized test scores Discipline referrals and behavior incidents	Positive and significant gains in academic achievement and social skills for students	http://studentsuccessskills.com/products/ready-learn-classroom-manual
Second Step (CG)	K–8	Social competence, bullying, and aggression	Teacher reports Student self-reports Survey information (related to increased awareness, knowledge, and skills) Behavior incident reports Attendance rates	Reduced behavior problems (drop in discipline referrals, bullying incidents, and improved report card grades related to conduct, effort, and behavior) Increased academic achievement (improved report card grades) Improved prosocial skills and social-competence knowledge	http://www.cfchildren.org/second-step/research

(Continued)

Table 5.1 (Continued)

Program/Curriculum (method of implementation)	Grade Level	Purpose/ Targeted Area of Improvement	Possible Perception and Results Data Sources	Evidenced Outcomes	Source
Student Success Skills (CG & SG)	4–12	Math ability Reading ability Behavioral outcomes Academic, social, and self-management skills Internal perceptions, emotions, and constructs	Teacher reports, student self-reports, survey information (related to increased awareness, knowledge, skills), standardized test scores, grades, behavior incidents, discipline referrals	Improved standardized test scores in reading and math Improvements in behavior (students maintain gains after two years) Increased knowledge Improved perceptions of classroom climate Increased engagement, motivation, and self-efficacy	Developer: http://www.studentsuccessskills.com
Too Good for Drugs (TGFD)	K–8	Increase social competence and problem-solving behavior Reduced at-risk factors and increased built-in protective factors	Teacher reports Student self-reports Observations Behavior incidents and discipline referrals	Positive effects on behavior, knowledge, attitudes, and values Higher levels of emotional-competency skills, social and resistance skills, goal-setting and decision-making skills, and prosocial behaviors Higher levels of perceptions of harmful effects of drugs and positive attitudes on the inappropriateness of drug use	https://www.toogoodprograms.org/too-good/evidence-base/

Program/Curriculum (method of implementation)	Grade Level	Purpose/ Targeted Area of Improvement	Possible Perception and Results Data Sources	Evidenced Outcomes	Source
				Later results evidence that the program is more effective with students at higher risk	
Too Good for Violence	K–12	Increase prosocial behaviors and protective factors related to conflict and violence	Teacher reports Student self-reports Observations Behavior incidents and discipline referrals	Higher emotional competency skills, social and conflict resolution skills, and communication skills More positive interactions with peers and fewer socially inappropriate behaviors	https://www.toogoodprograms.org/too-good/evidence-base/
Why Try (CG)	K–12	Social, emotional, and leadership skills that contribute to boosting resiliency	Teacher reports Student self-reports Survey information (related to increased awareness, knowledge, and skills) Student achievement (graduation rates, dropout rates, and GPA) Student behavior (discipline reports and incidents)	Reduced dropout rates Increased GPA Decreased expulsions Improved emotional health Reduced bullying behaviors and fighting Increased graduation rates Fewer emotional problems	http://whytry.org/index.php/component/content/article/79-resource-center/89-research-general

Note: CG = classroom guidance, SG = small group, IC = individual counseling

Table 5.2 Additional Resources

Resource	Website/Further Information
Centers for Disease Control and Prevention—Adolescent and School Health/Program Success Stories	http://www.cdc.gov/healthyyouth/stories/index.htm
Collaborative for Academic, Social, and Emotional Learning (CASEL) Effective Social Emotional Learning Programs	https://casel.squarespace.com/guide/ratings/elementary https://casel.squarespace.com/guide/programs http://www.casel.org/guide
National Registry of Evidence-based Programs and Practices (NREPP)	http://www.nrepp.samhsa.gov/ViewAll.aspx
Promising Practices Network—Archive on Children, Families, and Communities	http://www.promisingpractices.net/programs_outcome.asp
The Ron H. Frederickson Center for School Counseling Outcome Research & Evaluation	http://www.umass.edu/schoolcounseling
U.S. Department of Education—Office of Elementary and Secondary Education/Programs by Subject	http://www2.ed.gov/about/offices/list/oese/programsbysubject.html
The What Works Clearinghouse	http://ies.ed.gov/ncee/wwc

(Text continued from page 58)

then your delivery might fall flat. We provide some preliminary findings (simplified, of course) in Table 5.1. However, in order to best understand and grasp the overall design, implementation, and impact of these interventions, again we recommend that you go back to the original sources. A more specific example of research-based findings related to our sample goal is listed in Table 5.3.

The **fifth step** in our process covers logistical issues. Just because we have selected an intervention does not necessarily mean that we will be able to implement it. This is why this step is so critical! When you understand the research and evidence that backs your program as a viable intervention it is easier to "sell" it to your teachers, administrators, parents, and even your students. Dr. Greg Brigman, developer of the Student Success Skills (SSS) curriculum, refers to this as WIIFM—or, "What's in it for me?" If we begin

Table 5.3 Sample Table of Key Areas, Goals, Corresponding Data, Evidence-Based Programs, and Documented Outcomes

Key Areas/Topics	School Counseling Program Goals	Data to Be Collected	Evidence-Based Program to Be Delivered	Expected Outcomes/Effect Sizes for the Program
Bullying, harassment, gossip, rumors, sadness, and depression	Eighth-grade girls who scored in bottom 25% in math on their MAP assessment will increase these test scores by 10%	Winter and spring MAP scores	Student Success Skills (classroom and small-group programs)	Improvements in student academic achievement and behavior (i.e., increased prosocial skills, decreased bullying behaviors, and improved engagement) Positive perceptions of classroom climate Increases in standardized test scores in math and reading (overall ES of 0.29–0.41 math, 0.17 reading)

Note: MAP = Measures of Academic Progress, ES = effect size to frame how we approach our school counseling practice—and arguably our lives—from this lens, then we begin to communicate information in important, meaningful ways to our audience. Consider what the WIIFM may be for your teachers, administrators, and students prior to trying to get them on board with your program. In doing so, you will find that your schedule may become freed up for providing the types of services you had intended. You might also consider testing out or piloting the program first with a teacher or two with whom you already have a good working relationship. Planning for how things will go and how they actually go might be two different things, so we recommend you start small and make adjustments as needed. In terms of our example, we know that the SSS classroom program contains five weekly forty-five-minute classroom guidance lessons followed by three monthly forty-five-minute booster lessons, and the SSS small-group component consists of eight weekly forty-five-minute lessons. Given these logistics, is this a practical, doable intervention?

IMPLEMENT WITH FIDELITY

Finally, **Step 6** has to do with maintaining treatment fidelity. Evidence-based programs that are proven effective have stood the test of time and been subject to multiple studies that lend support to their use. Many of these programs are *manualized*, meaning a school counselor purchases materials that outline the program and then follows the manual step by step. Fidelity is increased if the school counselor attends a formal training on the use of the program as this increases the likelihood that the intervention will be implemented as it was originally designed. The critical piece in *tending to fidelity* has to do with delivering the program as it was intended to be delivered by the developer. Variations in implementation can result in variations in outcomes and decrease the school counselor's confidence in the salience of the intervention. Whenever possible, we strongly encourage you to adhere to each specific program's implementation standards. Furthermore, if you find this difficult, then we suggest you document the ways in which you have modified the delivery and understand and adjust for how these changes may impact your data.

Here is one more note regarding the implementation of evidence-based programs: Just because these types of interventions are preferred does not mean they are always realistic, possible, or will fit the needs of every student, counselor, or school site. Perhaps you have decided to get your feet wet by selecting one evidence-based program that you feel will really work well or benefit your students in some particular way. Begin with that one program, implement it to the best of your ability with fidelity, and continue to provide other services and interventions that you feel would work best in order to cover any other gaps or student needs. Perhaps these are lessons, activities, assemblies, or group plans that you have developed on your own. Fantastic! Do what works best for you, and build from there.

REFINE GOALS: STATE INTERVENTIONS AS A SUBPARAGRAPH TO THE GOAL

Here is the current rough draft of our goals:

Goal One

Eighth-grade females at our example middle school who receive the Student Success Skills (SSS) small-group-level intervention will increase their math achievement scores compared to eighth-grade females who do not receive SSS small-group intervention, as measured by MAP scores in fall, winter, and spring.

Goal Two

Eighth-grade students receiving free or reduced-cost meals who receive our intervention will increase their math achievement scores 10% more than their peers who do not receive our intervention, as measured by MAP scores in fall, winter, and spring.

ILLUSTRATING GOALS AND INTERVENTIONS IN LOGIC MODEL

Once an intervention has been chosen, whether it is an evidence-based intervention (hopefully) or a multitiered intervention currently in place you hope to evaluate, it can be inserted into the rectangle of the logic model. The intervention will be most effective if the intervention correlates specifically to the student-identified needs. Remember, the data indicator is not the problem, and the data indicator is not the solution. It is only one measure of success. Unfortunately, at this point in our educational system, the critical data elements are the "coin of the realm" and the language we will use to communicate the value of our program. However, *the true impact of our intervention occurs when we accurately and successfully match an intervention to a student-identified need.* The reciprocal relationship is indicated on the logic model in Figure 5.2 by a line with arrows on both sides. This goal is again illustrated using the visual for goal development in Figure 5.3.

Figure 5.2 Logic Model Illustrating Reciprocal Relationship Between Needs and Interventions

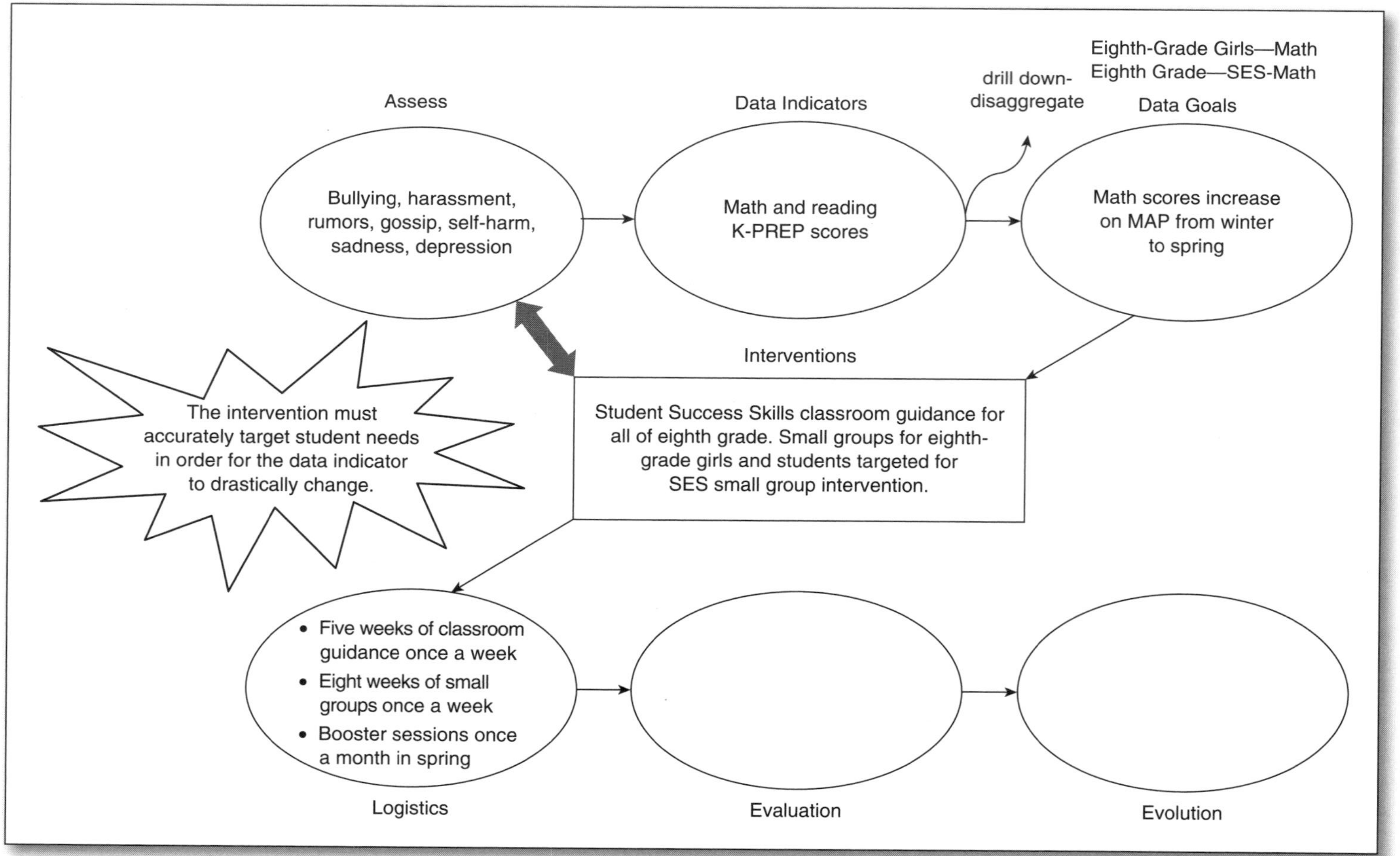

Eighth-Grade Girls—Math
Eighth Grade—SES-Math

Assess

Bullying, harassment, rumors, gossip, self-harm, sadness, depression

Data Indicators

Math and reading K-PREP scores

drill down-disaggregate

Data Goals

Math scores increase on MAP from winter to spring

The intervention must accurately target student needs in order for the data indicator to drastically change.

Interventions

Student Success Skills classroom guidance for all of eighth grade. Small groups for eighth-grade girls and students targeted for SES small group intervention.

- Five weeks of classroom guidance once a week
- Eight weeks of small groups once a week
- Booster sessions once a month in spring

Logistics

Evaluation

Evolution

Source: Adapted from Dimmitt, Carey, & Hatch (2007).

Figure 5.3 Visual for Goal Development

The Who (Specific Population You Are Targeting) Grade level, age, gender, any other *subgroup identifiers*	**My Who** Eighth-grade girls Eighth-grade students identified as free or reduced lunch
The What (Baseline Data—Be Specific) *Critical Data Elements* **Include cut-offs** (dates, scores, percentages—answer by when? by how much?)	**My What** KPREP scores from the previous year. However, to track the growth of our students over the year, we need a repeated measure. We use MAP in Kentucky. *Math scores from fall MAP assessment are our baseline.*
The How (Interventions and Logistics) Which *intervention*? Delivered when? At what level (**Tier 1, 2, or 3**)? For how long?	**My How** Tier 1 SSS and Tier 2 SSS small groups for both identified populations.
The Other What (Outcome/Target Increases) What will you know if the intervention is successful? How would **baseline data change**? What growth to what *outcomes*?	**My Other What** Math MAP scores assessed at both the winter evaluation and spring evaluation periods.

My Goal

Eighth-grade girls who scored at novice or apprentice the previous year on K-PREP or who scored in the lower 25% on the fall MAP evaluation will be targeted for Tier 2 Student Success Skills small groups and as a result will increase their MAP scores on the spring math MAP evaluation by 10% more than peers not receiving the SSS small groups.

Notice that my goal names the intervention and creates a comparison, whether that comparison data point is to a previous score period (e.g., fall math MAP scores) or to a comparison group (e.g., other eighth-grade females not receiving the small-group intervention). Choose the data process that is the easiest to use, or use both if possible. Once we begin to implement multiple interventions, it may seem difficult to keep track of everything being done through the school counseling program. A previous student created a visual we termed an *umbrella* to illustrate all the school counseling interventions occurring under the umbrella of a specific ASCA domain.

ORGANIZING INTERVENTIONS USING UMBRELLAS

Now that you understand the process to follow for selecting appropriate evidence-based interventions, you may find that you have become quite a popular person on campus. Administrators, colleagues, and parents have seen what you can do, and they want more of it. However, as your comprehensive program grows, things can also get complicated, so finding ways to organize items can help. Umbrellas can be useful tools. School counseling interventions and guidance curriculum can be sorted and checked using umbrellas to make sure they cover all three of the ASCA domains—academic, social/emotional, and career—for all students in your school. (You might also find the RAMP ASCA Student Standards Program Planning Tool helpful at this point.) For example, an elementary school counselor responsible for students in Grades K–5 should be able to demonstrate how they are providing programming for students in these key areas. This can be a hefty task. Organizing school counseling efforts using umbrellas provides an easy visual representation of interventions so that the counselor can see where programming is comprehensive and where, perhaps, it is lacking. Begin by listing your programs and interventions in a table format (see Tables 5.4 and 5.5).

Table 5.4 Blank Interventions Table by Domain

Grade Level	Academic	Career	Social/Emotional

Table 5.5 Interventions Table by Domain

Grade Level	Academic	Career	Social/Emotional
5	Student Success Skills (SSS)		
5		Career Day Reality Store	
5			Character Counts Positive Behavioral Interventions and Supports (PBIS) Student Success Skills (SSS)

List all possible services facilitated or delivered by the school counseling department (see Table 5.5). Next, organize these interventions by using umbrellas (academic, social/emotional, and career). On the next page, Figure 5.4 shows a blank template for the social/emotional domain, and Figure 5.5 shows a completed umbrella for the social/emotional domain. Templates for all three domain areas can be accessed in the online resource center (http://www.corwin.com/ZyromskiEvidenceBased).

TIPS AND TRICKS

Several of the schools we work with have found that using one housing document that lists interventions, target groups, implementation time frames, data, and outcomes makes things easier, particularly when working toward RAMP certification. Containing this information in one easy planning tool permits counselors to pull items into the specific RAMP templates at a later date. We call this planning tool the "School Counseling Program Goal-Tracking Form," which can also be found in the online resource center (http://www.corwin.com/ZyromskiEvidenceBased).

FULFILLING COMPONENTS OF RAMP

Many of the planning tools outlined in this chapter will prove useful in your RAMP application process. Selecting evidence-based programs that have

Figure 5.4 Blank Umbrella Template With One Example

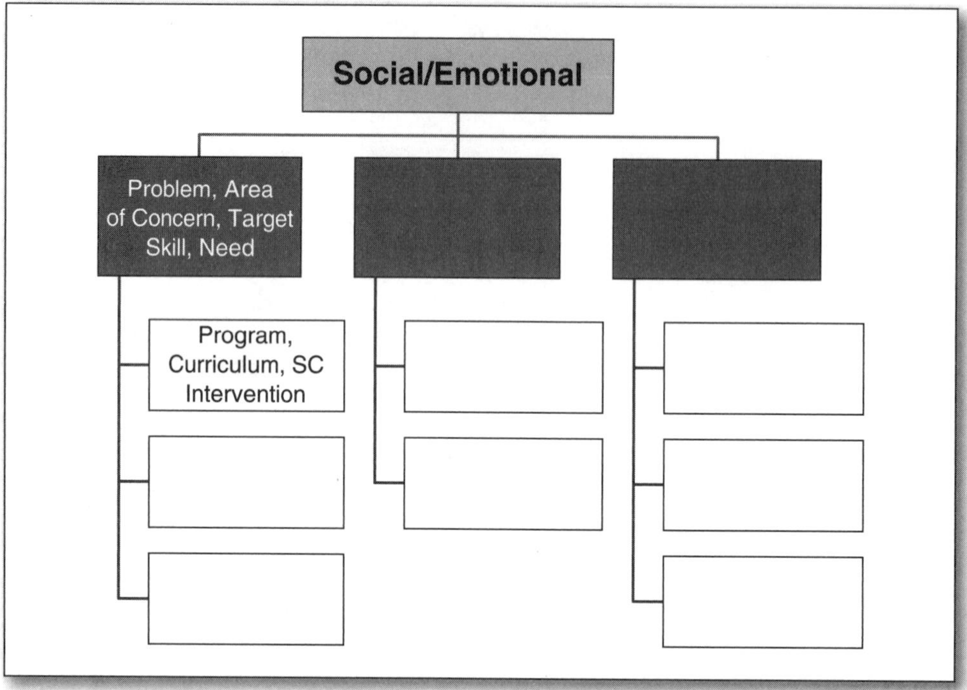

Figure 5.5 Umbrella Template With Multiple Interventions Inserted

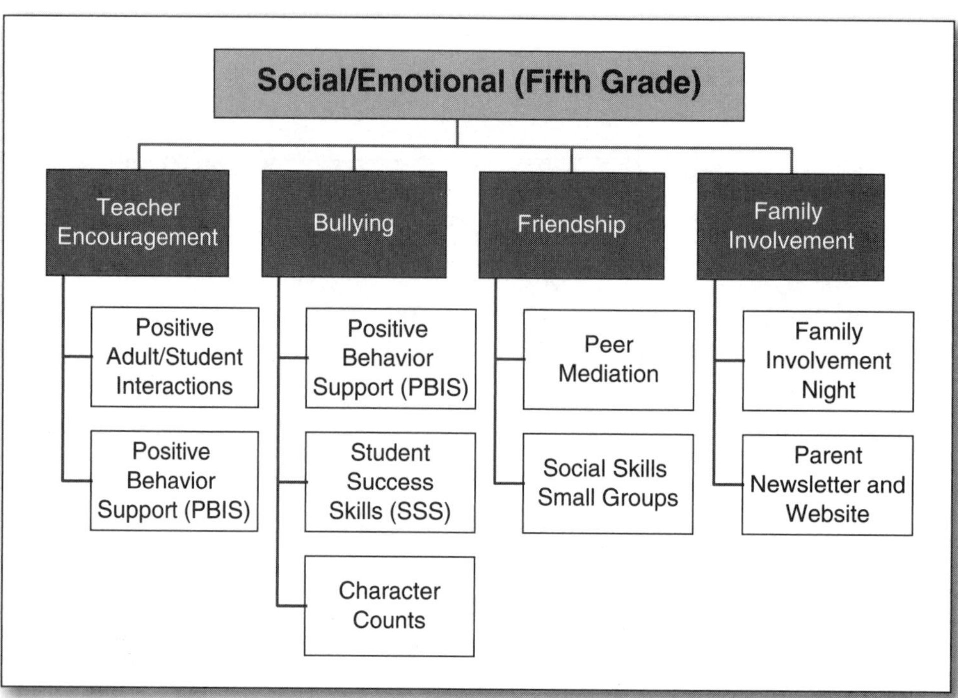

been tied to specific social, emotional, academic, and behavioral gains for students seems logical. School counselors must articulate and provide reasoning for the evidence-based programs they choose to implement in the following RAMP templates and corresponding narratives: (1) School Counseling Program Goals, (2) Annual Agreement, (3) School Counseling Core Curriculum Action Plan, (4) Small-Group Responsive Services (5) Closing-the-Gap Results Report, and (6) Program Evaluation Reflection. Intentionally choosing evidence-based interventions assists the school counselor in identifying suitable target populations, noting corresponding areas of concern, filtering down primary school counseling goals, and determining what outcomes to investigate.

6 Evaluation and Evolution

A Checklist for Evaluating and Evolving Your Program	
Completed?	**Processes (including any necessary materials)**
❒	Answer the principal evaluation questions (*the what, why, how, and when*).
❒	Determine appropriate evaluations that align with your programs, curriculum, services, and interventions. (*Are these measures valid and reliable?*)
❒	Collect your data at multiple time frames. *(Create pre- and post-assessments.)*
❒	Establish baseline data. (*Take a snapshot.*)
❒	Use Excel (or a similar program) to organize and analyze your data.
❒	Determine what your findings suggest (*trends and future courses of action*).

PURPOSE OF EVALUATION AND EVOLUTION

Why evaluate? Simply, we need to determine if the things we are doing each day matter. We need to provide accountability. Do we make a difference, positive or negative, for our students? Are students truly impacted as a result of our efforts? The only way we can answer these questions is if we collect evidence of our effectiveness, analyze that data, and report on it. School counseling program evaluation is an ongoing process that assesses both the delivery of services (process data) and outcomes (product evaluation). In this way, evaluation helps drive our school counseling programming decisions.

Looking back at the logic model, we see that evaluation and evolution are our last step and help circle us back to where we started: assessing our program. Note the cyclical nature of our logic model (see Figure 6.1). The only way to cycle back and determine appropriate revisions to our current program, set new goals, and so forth is to evaluate. Thus, evaluation is the key to evolution.

Evaluation serves several purposes for school counselors, administrators, and other important stakeholders. For one, it assists counselors in determining the impact of their services on students, staff, and the overall school climate. In addition, evaluating permits counselors to see if they are making progress in accomplishing their school counseling program goals. If progress is not being made—or not being made in the time frame it was predicted to change in—then school counselors can adjust their goals and correct course. Evaluation also benefits counselors as it provides direction on what components

Figure 6.1 Process for Building Evidence-Based School Counseling Program

ASSESS
Reciprocal Relationship
GOALS
Apply LOGIC MODEL
INTERVENTIONS
Organize With Umbrellas
EVALUATION AND EVOLUTION

- Report Card
- School Improvement Plan
- Needs Assessments
- Evaluation Results

- 2–3 per Year
- Prioritize
- Drill Down

- Evidence-Based
- Targeted
- Relevant

- Data Analysis
- Evolve Infrastructure

Beliefs
Mission
Vision

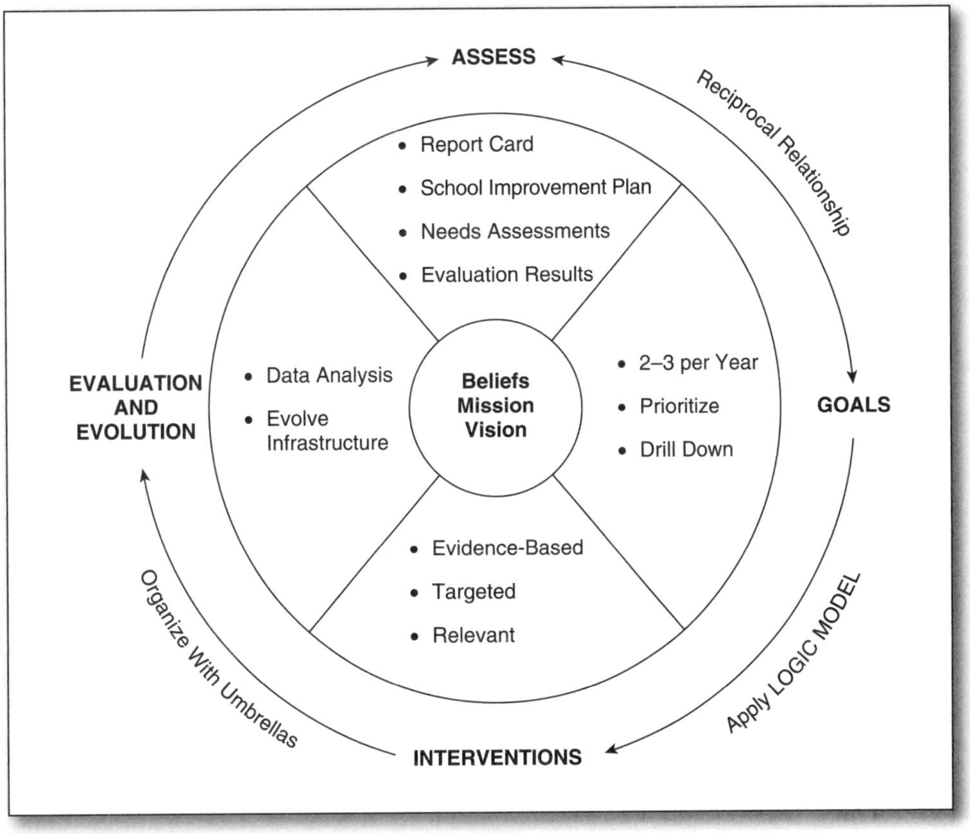

Note: The arrows indicate the reciprocal relationship of various aspects of the process.

of the program are working and which are not. Finally, when counselors evaluate, they are better able to identify gaps in their own professional development and what resources they may be lacking. Adapting and refining the school counseling program to best fit student needs should be the end goal.

School counselors can use evaluation practices to investigate several aspects of their program. Are the evidence-based interventions you selected resulting in measurable, positive outcomes for students? Does your program meet program standards? When you consult with parents and teachers, do these meetings result in improved services for students? Will students overcome behavioral and academic challenges as a result of your efforts? Are you performing adequately in your role as an advocate and supporter for all students? Big or small, evaluation provides answers to these key questions. ASCA provides a quick monitoring tool for practitioners to use that can help guide certain aspects of program evaluation. This Excel document, titled "School Counseling Program Assessment," can be found in the online resource center (http://www.corwin.com/ZyromskiEvidenceBased).

DESIGNING EVALUATION

Now that we understand the critical importance of evaluation, we can begin to design our evaluation system. In previous chapters, we determined ***what*** we were going to measure (*data source—perception or results, preferably a critical data element is included*) and ***why*** we were going to measure it (*outcomes that are linked to the program we selected*). In this chapter, we will decide ***how*** we are going to measure the outcome(s) and ***when*** we are going to capture our data in order to determine if changes, growth, or improvements have occurred. We will also discuss how much change we can expect for our data goals.

Evaluation can be a daunting process—one that can very easily become overwhelming. Many school counselors shy away from evaluation because they do not feel adequately trained in or prepared for it. Try not to fall victim to this mindset. Evaluation is both necessary and integral to your continued success. **So let's start small. Focus on one goal and one intervention at a time.** Go back and refer to the outcomes we listed related to the evidence-based program selected in Chapter 5. Remember that critical data elements (those items referred to in a school's or district's report card, including graduation, attendance, and discipline rates; school grades; test scores; and enrollment numbers) carry the most weight with administrators and school leaders. In our example, we listed MAP standardized test scores as the results-based or critical data element to be collected. We know the ***what***, so let's take a moment to look at ***why*** it is that we have selected this outcome. Can this data element be linked to the evidence-based program we selected? The answer is yes, we can confirm research that supports the effectiveness of the SSS program to positively improve student standardized test scores in math and reading. Next, we must consider ***how*** we set the criteria for the changes we anticipate seeing. Are we expecting an increase or decrease in behavior or performance? Will we measure this change or growth in terms of points, scaled scores, total scores, observable behaviors, or self-reported perceptions or feelings?

Chapter 5 highlighted the value of selecting evidence-based programs for their research base supporting the impact they have on certain student outcomes. Connecting our interventions to outcomes and outcomes to interventions should go hand in hand. Back to our example, we had yet to determine the amount of change to expect in our goal. Since we are using Measures of Academic Progress (MAP) to track the behavior change in math scores for our eighth-grade students, we can obtain the average growth for MAP between the fall, winter, and spring testing periods. For example, eighth-grade fall-to-winter average growth is two points. Thus, even a 10% gain beyond average growth for the eighth grade would be less than one point. If students on grade level obtain an average of a two-point gain, we can hope that our students gain at least one point. For example, using our previous goal but tweaking it to use normed MAP growth as our comparison, the goal might be written as follows:

> Eighth-grade females at our example middle school who receive Tier 2 small-group counseling interventions will increase their math achievement score by 10% more than the normed growth on math MAP for eighth-grade students.

A second way to write a similar goal, keeping the comparison with other eighth-grade females, might be written in the following way:

> Eighth-grade females at our example middle school who receive Tier 2 small-group counseling intervention will increase their math achievement scores by 10% more than eighth-grade females who do not receive our intervention, as measured by MAP scores in fall, winter, and spring.

Standardized assessments, such as the Measures of Academic Progress test, are considered to be valid and reliable sources of data. MAP is a standards-based adaptive assessment that generates data related to student growth in reading, language, and math over time (more about that later). As discussed in Chapter 3, though process and perception data are useful, we are most interested in data that reflects behavior change (results data). Standardized test scores meet this criteria as they are reflective of changes in academic achievement.

When deciding which assessments to employ, keep in mind that quality matters. Though we put much stock into standardized tests, alternative forms of measurement (questionnaires, surveys, self-reports, and peer nominations), including those that assess perceptual data (pre- and post-assessments of knowledge, attitudes, perceptions, and competencies), can also provide useful information. However, when possible, you should choose instruments that are both valid and reliable. No big statistics lecture is needed here other than to say that an instrument is considered valid if it truly measures what it set out to measure (face, construct, and criterion) and reliable if it gives you similar results when you repeatedly measure the same unchanged construct. If an instrument were perfectly reliable, then it would have a perfect positive ($r = +1$) correlation with the true scores. As a rule of thumb, reliability estimates (reported as alpha coefficients) of 0.70 or higher are preferred. Table 6.1 provides a sample list of recommended instruments and assessments and the corresponding constructs they assess. You may select assessments from this list (assuming they align with the constructs you are investigating) or choose your own.

The instruments listed in Table 6.1 are especially valuable in measuring changes in behavior as well as knowledge, perceptions, and skills related to behavior change. To clarify, this table contains instruments that have already been tested and proven effective. This does not mean that you cannot develop your own simple assessments in order to gauge perception data from your students, teachers, parents, or others. *Developing quick and simple pre- and post-assessments as they relate to changes in thoughts, feelings, attitudes, knowledge, skills, and perceptions are encouraged, particularly if they relate to your specific school counseling program goals.* And though we recommend that you get into the practice of collecting multiple sources of data, you do not need to collect perceptual data every time you implement an intervention, which brings us to our last consideration. In our evaluation process, we must also decide the ***when***—the time frames we designate as to when we will collect our data. This leads us to further discussion on pre- and post-assessments and the value of baseline data.

ABOUT PRE- AND POST-ASSESSMENTS

Collecting data at various points in time is smart practice. Practitioners can use the information generated from pre- and post-assessments to measure the perceptions of key stakeholders. Hatch (2014) suggests that if we are wondering whether or not students have learned anything as a result of our counseling efforts that we "ASK" them, using this acronym to indicate

(Text continued on page 86)

Table 6.1 Sample List of Instruments for Assessing School-Based Curricula, Programs, and Interventions

Name	Author(s)	Area of Interest	Grade Level/Age	Psychometrics
Aggression Scale	Orpinas and Frankowski (2001); Orpinas, Horne, and Staniszewski (2003)	Eleven-item measure assessing frequency of self-reported perpetration of teasing, pushing, or threatening others	Ages 10–15	Cronbach's alpha: 0.88 to 0.90
Bullying-Behavior Scale	Austin and Joseph (1996)	Six-item student self-assessment of events (including acts of bullying and/or victimization) that might happen in school	Ages 8–11	Cronbach's alpha: 0.82
Child Behavior Rating Scale (CBRS)	Bronson, Goodson, Layzer, and Love (1990)	Teacher assessment of student behavioral self-regulation—ability to manage one's own behavior in academic and social settings	Kindergarten	Very good internal consistency and test-retest reliability Internal consistency coefficients Cronbach's alphas range from 0.69 to 0.97, and two- to four-week test-retest reliability coefficients range from 0.56 to 0.96 (all correlations significant, $p < .001$) Inter-rater reliability coefficients range from 0.50 to 0.89 (all correlations significant, $p < .001$) Convergent and divergent validity supported

(Continued)

Table 6.1 (Continued)

Name	Author(s)	Area of Interest	Grade Level/Age	Psychometrics
Children's Social Behavior Scale–Self-Report	Crick and Grotpeter (1995)	Fifteen-item measure with six subscales assessing the relative frequency of various types of aggressive and prosocial behaviors and loneliness	Ages 8–14	Cronbach's alpha: Overt aggression = 0.94 Relational aggression = 0.83 Prosocial behavior = 0.91 Loneliness = 0.92
Five Factor Wellness Inventory Form T (5F-Wel-T)	Myers and Sweeney (2005)	Student assessment of characteristics of wellness; measures the total wellness or the entirety of the indivisible self	Grade 6 and above	Alphas range from 0.90 to 0.94, with an alpha of 0.94 for total wellness
Iowa Test of Basic Skills	Hoover, Dunbar, and Frisbie (2001)	Student standardized measure of vocabulary, reading comprehension, spelling, capitalization, punctuation, usage and expression, math concepts and estimation, math problem solving and data interpretation, math computation, social studies, maps and diagrams, reference materials, word analysis (Level 9 only), and listening (Level 9 only)	Grades K–12	Norm-referenced; norms allow you to compare student performance with that of a representative sample of students across the country with current information

Name	Author(s)	Area of Interest	Grade Level/Age	Psychometrics
Junior Meta-Cognition Awareness Inventory (Jr. MAI)	Sperling, Howard, Miller, and Murphy (2002)	Student self-report inventory that measures likelihood to think about one's thoughts in a given circumstance	Grades 3–5	Cronbach's alpha: 0.87, high internal consistency
Multidimensional Peer-Victimization Scale	Mynard and Joseph (2000)	Student self-report across four subscales assessing physical and verbal victimization, social manipulation, and property attacks	Ages 11–16	Internal consistency: Physical victimization = 0.85 Verbal victimization = 0.75 Social manipulation = 0.77 Property attacks = 0.73
My Class Inventory—Short Form Revised (MCI-SFR)	Sink and Spencer (2005)	Assesses student perceptions of various aspects of classroom climate: satisfaction, friction, difficulty, cohesion, and competitiveness	Grades 4–6	Alpha coefficients for each of the scales range from 0.84 to 0.93.
My Class Inventory—Short Form for Teachers (TMCI-SF)	Sink and Spencer (2007)	Assesses overall teacher perceptions of their present classroom experience: satisfaction, friction, competitiveness, difficulty, cohesion, and counselor impact	Elementary	Alpha reliabilities ranging from 0.58 to 0.93 (SCI; M_{α} = 0.78)
Olweus Bullying Questionnaire	Solberg and Olweus (2003)	Thirty-nine-item measure assessing the frequency of bully perpetration and victimization	Ages 11–17	Cronbach's alpha: Bully perpetration = 0.88 Bully victimization = 0.87

(Continued)

Table 6.1 (Continued)

Name	Author(s)	Area of Interest	Grade Level/Age	Psychometrics
Positive Youth Development Questionnaire—Short Version	Lerner et al. (2005)	SHORT PYD student questionnaire measures the five *Cs* (competence, connection, confidence, caring, and character)	Ages 10 and up	Cronbach's alphas range between 0.63 and 0.90
Social Skills Rating Scale (SSRS)	Gresham and Elliot (2007)	Screen and classify children and adolescents suspected of having social behavior problems. Students rate themselves on aspects related to teacher–student relationships, peer acceptance, and academic performance by assessing both positive and problem social behaviors	Ages 8–18	Strong internal consistency and test-retest reliability Coefficient alphas in the upper 0.90s Median subscale reliabilities are in the high 0.80s for the Teacher Form, the mid-0.80s for the Parent Form, and near 0.80 for the Student Form All alpha coefficients are equal to or exceed 0.70
Stanford Achievement Test Series (SAT10)	Pearson (2012)	Student standardized measure of reading, reading comprehension, mathematics, language, spelling, listening comprehension, science, and social studies	Grades K–12	Norm-referenced; norms allow you to compare student performance with that of a representative sample of students across the country with current information

Name	Author(s)	Area of Interest	Grade Level/Age	Psychometrics
Student Engagement in School Success Skills (SESSS)	Carey, Brigman, Webb, Villares, and Harrington (2013)	Student self-report of cognitive engagement of Student Success Skills (SSS) program skills and strategies	Grades 4–12	Coefficient alphas for the three SESSS subscales: Self-direction of learning = 0.89 Support of classmates' learning = 0.79 Self-regulation of arousal = 0.68 0.90 for the SESSS as a whole (Villares, Colvin, Carey, Webb, Brigman, & Harrington, 2014), indicating good internal consistency
Student Participation Questionnaire (SPQ)	Finn, Folger, and Cox (1991)	Teacher rating scale used to assess four subscales representing four key themes of social participation: friendships/relationships, contacts/interactions, student's social self-perception, and acceptance by classmates	Grades K–1	Coefficient alphas ranging from 0.89–0.94

(Text continued from page 80)

assessment of the ASCA Standards of **A**ttitudes (what students believe), **S**kills (what they can demonstrate), and **K**nowledge (what they know). Dr. Tim Poynton always says the first step in survey development is to "avoid making a survey." In other words, know which surveys or pre-posts are going to benefit the students and your program. If an already established instrument (valid and reliable) exists, use it! However, if an instrument does not exist (or is not reasonable or doable in terms of cost or time) but collecting information on whatever construct or intervention is still of interest to you, then consider developing your own. Again, keep things simple; developing one quick five- or six-item pre-post survey that reflects one of your school counseling goals will do for now. You can always build from there. Some suggestions to keep in mind when developing pre-posts are as follows:

- Forced responses such as yes or no or Likert scale–type answers (strongly agree, agree, disagree, or strongly disagree) are preferred over essay, short answer, or fill-in-the-blank responses, as they can be easily converted (or *coded*) into numerical values for later analysis.
- Keep the language simple and straightforward and refrain from asking multiple questions at a time.
- Pilot test your survey. Administer it to a focus group of students, teachers, or parents, and gather their feedback.
- Consider developing the assessment in an electronic format. This will help save you time, immensely, when it comes to inputting and analyzing your results.

A sample pre-/post-assessment is shown in Figure 6.2.

Electronic formats can be created using Google Docs (http://www.google.com/docs/about/) or a survey tool, such as SurveyMonkey (http://www.surveymonkey.com) or Zoomerang (https://www.zoomerang.com). Some sample pre-/post-surveys that have been created by practitioners can be found in the online resource center (http://www.corwin.com/ZyromskiEvidenceBased). Others created and used by practitioners can be found on Hatch's website hatchingresults.com in the online appendix of "The Use of Data in School Counseling" (http://hatchingresults.com/books/Use-Of-Data/online-appendix.cfm).

CREATING BASELINES

So how do we know if the interventions we provide truly make a difference if we don't determine a baseline for student functioning prior to that intervention? Can we attribute any change, positive or negative, to our school counseling

Figure 6.2 Sample Pre-/Post-Test for Ready to Learn

Ready to Learn: Pre-/Post-Test for Teachers

Student Name: ______________________ Grade: ______________________

Date: ______________ Teacher Name: ______________________

Directions: Circle the BEST answer.

1. On average, my students pay attention in class.
   A. Most of the time
   B. Sometimes
   C. Never
2. On average, my students sit still.
   A. Most of the time
   B. Sometimes
   C. Never
3. On average, my students look at me (make eye contact) during class discussion.
   A. Most of the time
   B. Sometimes
   C. Never
4. On average, my students ask relevant (effective) questions.
   A. Most of the time
   B. Sometimes
   C. Never
5. On average, my students try hard and don't give up on tasks even if the tasks are difficult for them.
   A. Most of the time
   B. Sometimes
   C. Never

efforts if we do not know what was happening prior to the start of those efforts? Some counselors have asked us if they need to collect pre-tests or if a post-test alone will suffice. Our answer is simple—it's best to collect data from both points in time. Simply put, pre-tests provide us with a baseline. Gathering baseline data—data that captures information at a certain point in time prior to the addition of any intentional modifications to our programming—is a key part in the process. Referring back to our example, we note that the collection of MAP scores is particularly useful in that this assessment is administered three times a year (fall, winter, and spring), providing educators with valuable data at multiple intervals. *True evaluation takes place when notable differences occur from one point in time to another point in time, preferably before the intervention occurs and after it has been implemented.* **If we do not capture data at**

both points in time, we cannot confidently attribute changes we see to the particular program or service we delivered.

Baselines vary depending upon the outcomes you are tracking on, and evidenced impact may depend upon the baseline criteria that you establish. For instance, going back to our example, we could have established our baseline data criteria according to (a) student progress made from the previous school year's MAP scores, (b) student progress made between the three MAP testing periods (fall, winter, spring) within the same school year, or (c) student progress made between these various intervals for specified students, groups of students, classrooms of students, or grade levels of students. Depending upon how we set this up and what we are interested in assessing (i.e., hopefully whether or not a school counseling intervention or service we delivered positively affected student performance on this assessment), the baseline data we collect will vary. Looking at our example, we planned to collect baseline data from the fall MAP assessment, then implement our SSS classroom intervention (Tier 1) and collect winter MAP data, then implement our SSS small-group intervention (Tier 2) and collect spring MAP data (see Figure 6.3 for a visual representation of this analysis).

Figure 6.3 Visual Representation of Analysis

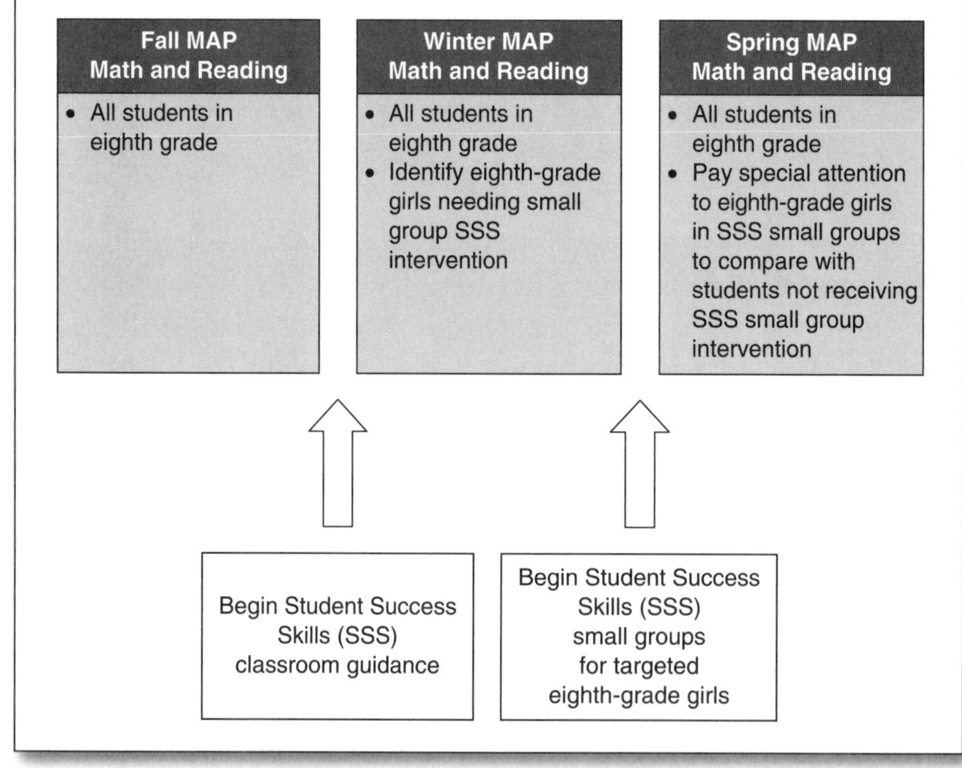

Doing things in this manner permits us to assess whether any gains made could be attributed to our delivery. Another consideration would be to compare these gains between testing intervals to gains made between intervals in the year prior, when a school counseling intervention was not delivered. What gains (or setbacks) did these same students make in that year as compared to this one? We would also compare the gains by the females participating in the small group with those not participating in the small group. What gains (or setbacks) did the females in the group make compared to females not in the group? How do we explain these gains or setbacks? (We'll use this to evolve our intervention later.) As you can see, variations in your evaluation criteria can impact the results you see, but if we fail to set an accurate baseline, one that does not truly reflect student performance prior to the addition of our intervention, then we can't confidently attribute student changes to anything we have done. This is why careful consideration of the ***when*** is so critical.

ORGANIZING DATA: EXCEL SPREADSHEETS

We know that simply reading the word *Excel* may be causing you some unwanted anxiety, but take a breath. We are going to walk you through everything you need to know about creating, organizing, and effectively managing your data using Excel spreadsheets. To the novice practitioner, Excel can seem more complicated than it actually is. We are going to simplify what you need to know by narrowing down the information you need to input into three categories: (1) *demographic information*, (2) *critical data elements*, and (3) *interventions*. Demographic information includes items like student numbers, grade level, gender, and ethnicity. Your critical data elements are the results-based data outcomes we have been referring to which are of particular interest to administrators (standardized test scores, attendance rates, and graduation rates). Lastly, the interventions column lists the programs and services you delivered. Please make note that providing a ***key*** allows for us to assign a numerical value (which does pertain to a number really) to any type of information (descriptive or not) that we input.

Using a key is very important. For example, below (see Figure 6.4), the number *4* is used to denote students who received multitiered interventions (classroom guidance, small group, and individual counseling), though this does not necessarily signify that this is "better" or of "higher" value than those students entered as *1* who just received classroom intervention. Note also that though our gender column contains letters (*F* and *M*), these might also be coded using numeric values (perhaps *1* and *2*). Take some time to create separate spreadsheets by grade level, classroom, or small group.

Figure 6.4 Excel Spreadsheet Setup With Data

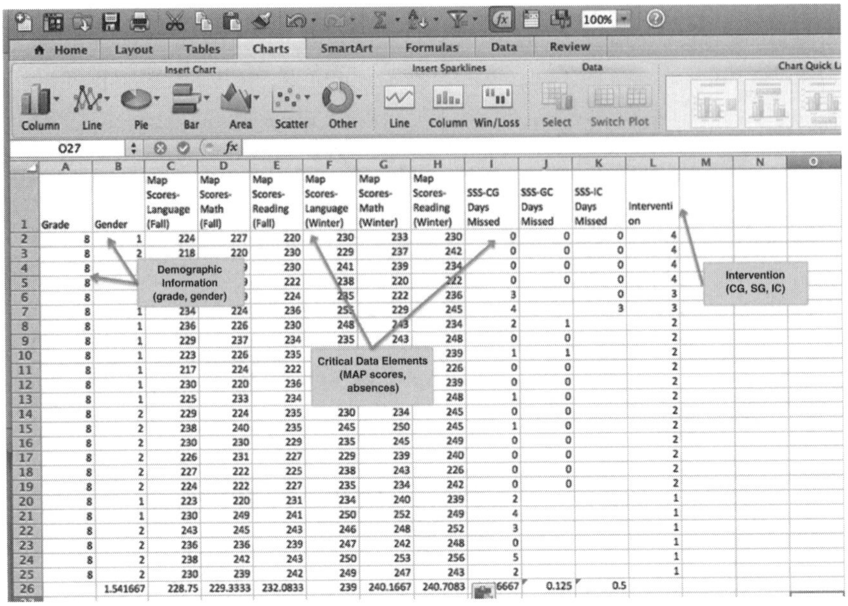

	A	B	C	D	E	F	G	H	I	J	K	L
1	Grade	Gender	Map Scores-Language (Fall)	Map Scores-Math (Fall)	Map Scores-Reading (Fall)	Map Scores-Language (Winter)	Map Scores-Math (Winter)	Map Scores-Reading (Winter)	SSS-CG Days Missed	SSS-GC Days Missed	SSS-IC Days Missed	Intervention
2	8	1	224	227	220	230	233	230	0	0	0	4
3	8	2	218	220	230	229	237	242	0	0	0	4
4	8	[illegible]	[illegible]	[illegible]	230	241	239	234	0	0	0	4
5	8	[illegible]	[illegible]	[illegible]	222	238	220	222	0	0	0	4
6	8	[illegible]	[illegible]	[illegible]	224	235	222	236	3		0	3
7	8	1	234	224	236	255	229	245	4		3	3
8	8	1	236	226	230	248	243	234	2	1		2
9	8	1	229	237	234	235	243	248	0	0		2
10	8	1	223	226	235	[illegible]	[illegible]	239	1	1		2
11	8	1	217	224	222	[illegible]	[illegible]	226	0	0		2
12	8	1	230	220	236	[illegible]	[illegible]	239	0	0		2
13	8	1	225	233	234	[illegible]	[illegible]	248	1	0		2
14	8	2	229	224	235	230	234	245	0	0		2
15	8	2	238	240	235	245	250	245	1	0		2
16	8	2	230	230	229	235	245	249	0	0		2
17	8	2	226	231	227	229	239	240	0	0		2
18	8	2	227	222	225	238	243	226	0	0		2
19	8	2	224	222	227	235	234	242	0	0		2
20	8	1	223	220	231	234	240	239	2			1
21	8	1	230	249	241	250	252	249	4			1
22	8	2	243	245	243	246	248	252	3			1
23	8	2	236	236	239	247	242	248	0			1
24	8	2	238	242	243	250	253	256	5			1
25	8	2	230	239	242	249	247	243	2			1
26		1.541667	228.75	229.3333	232.0833	239	240.1667	240.7083	[illegible]6667	0.125	0.5	

Demographic Information (grade, gender)
Critical Data Elements (MAP scores, absences)
Intervention (CG, SG, IC)

(This may help you later with copying and pasting.) Figure 6.4 is a screenshot example of how to set up an Excel spreadsheet with these three categories and a corresponding key.

Now that your spreadsheet is set up, take some time to review your data. Check for missing values as well as any outliers (e.g., blank cells or numbers that seem "off"). Next, determine what to do with this problematic data if you discover it. Do you have a way to go back and check the original assessments, school-level reports, or your own records to confirm the values entered? If you do, excellent! Go back to the original source, double-check your entries, and modify as needed. But if you don't have the original data to go back to, then decide what you will do with those items prior to analysis (determine a scoring protocol, document it, and stick to it) as including "problem data" can throw off your results significantly.

ANALYSIS

Now that you have your data cleaned up, you can begin to sort it. You may choose to sort the data according to different criteria (e.g., gender or absentees). However, since we are most interested in the impact of our school counseling interventions, we recommend you begin here. Remember, the information you provided in your ***key*** tells us who received which interventions. Using the Sort option in the Data tab (top-left corner; see the screen shot in Figure 6.5), click into the "Intervention" column and click Sort. This will refile all of your data by intervention category (CG, SG, and IC). Going back to our example, recall that we were interested in determining if the eighth-grade females who received the SSS small-group program would improve on their MAP scores from fall to winter. In order to analyze the correct information, we must begin by disaggregating our data by who received our intervention (SSS, CG, and SG).

Once you do this, ***double-check and make sure that ALL of the data in your spreadsheet gets sorted and not just that specific column***. Now you can begin to copy and paste the data you are interested in analyzing into additional separate spreadsheets. For instance, we are interested in analyzing change scores from fall testing periods for MAP to winter testing periods for MAP, so we would copy and paste those corresponding columns into separate spreadsheets by intervention group (in our case, by students who received the SSS small-group intervention). Take some time to review your initial analyses, and note particular trends, increases, decreases, gender disparities, and so forth. Running some descriptive statistics on your data set can also point you toward these findings (refer to Figure 6.6). By computing change scores between fall and winter MAPs, we can see that the majority of students increased their scores by at least one point in language, math, and reading. (Those in our treatment group are highlighted yellow.) Remember, all students in this class received the SSS classroom

Figure 6.5 Data, Sort Function

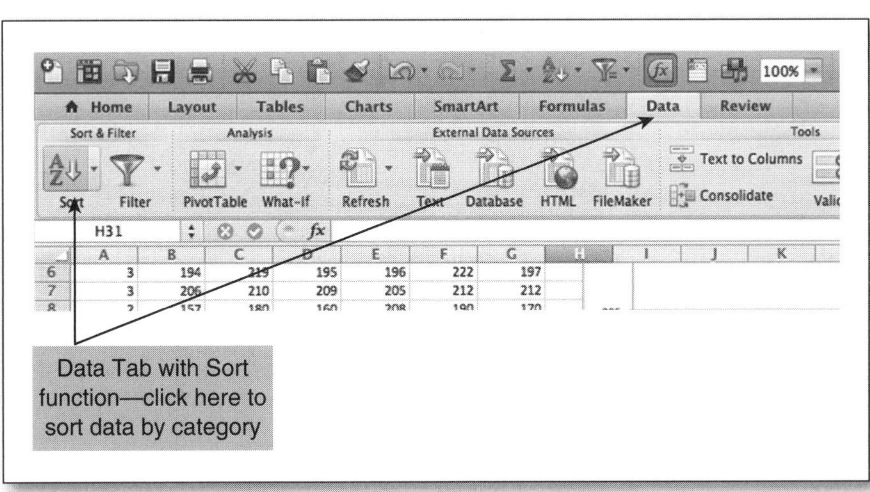

Figure 6.6 Change Scores MAP and Trends

Intervention	Change Score MAP in Language	Change Score MAP in Math	Change Score in MAP in Reading
4	6	6	8
4	6	9	5
4	9	4	4
4	8	1	0
3	3	3	3
3	8	5	9
2	9	4	4
2	6	3	4
2	1	8	4
2	7	4	4
2	9	4	3
2	10	9	4
2	1	6	5
2	7	7	2
2	5	9	10
2	3	8	3
2	9	7	1
2	6	5	5
1	4	5	8
1	5	3	8
1	3	3	9
1	5	6	6
1	0	10	6
1	2	8	1
		12/12 improved	

intervention. However, students in yellow received both the SSS classroom and small-group interventions. Many students in this subgroup evidenced significant increases across all three areas. In our sample goal, we were interested in math scores, and we can see that those students in yellow increased their scores in math anywhere from three to nine points! As you will see later (in Figure 6.12), the average increase in math MAP scores from fall to winter for students who receive "regular educational programming" (i.e., no supplemental counseling interventions) make average gains of about three points.

Next, you will want to find the average of each column using the correct formula (see Figure 6.7). Additional, more complex formulas can be utilized in Excel as well, but remember, we are keeping it simple (see "Tips and Tricks").

Figure 6.7 Average Formula in Excel

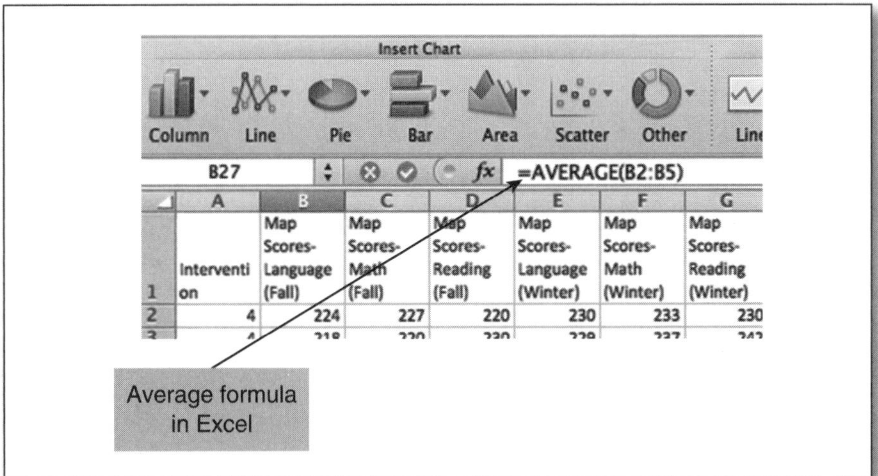

TIPS AND TRICKS

The EZAnalyze software is an Excel add-in that can drastically save you time and energy in your data entry, organization, analysis, and creation of results reports and visuals. Here is even better news: This software is completely FREE and available for download at www.ezanalyze.com/download/index.htm.

Dr. Russell Sabella has also created a data and analysis system of his own. The tutorial is designed to provide you with step-by-step instructions for learning tips, tricks, and shortcuts when dealing with data in your work. Visit Data Boot Camp 2.0 at www.mydatabootcamp.com.

Jeremy Goldman, school counselor at Pikesville High School, among others, has posted helpful Excel tutorials about how to create spreadsheets on YouTube at www.youtube.com/watch?v=NcT2dbcBt88.

If you wish to pay for programs that provide tracking tools, you can check out programs such as School Counselor Central at schoolcounselorcentral.com or Redesigning School Counseling at cgi.asainstitute.org/cgi-bin/rsc/intro.

Now that you have averages for each column, take those averages and list them adjacent to one another, labeling them with the correct headings (see Figure 6.8).

As you can see, we have pulled only the students who received the SSS classroom intervention followed by the SSS small-group intervention and pulled their average scores from their fall and winter MAPs for language, math, and reading. This information is now labeled appropriately, and we can highlight it and click to create charts and graphs from there. For example, Figures 6.9 and 6.10 are both visual representations of this data, represented in both a bar graph and a line graph. As you can see, students who received the SSS small-group intervention made noticeable gains across

Figure 6.8 Data and Criteria Setup for Graphs, Charts, and Visuals

36								
37	CG & SG	Fall	Winter			language	math	reading
38	language	229.92	242.25		Fall	229.92	224.25	230.25
39	math	224.25	227.5		Winter	242.25	227.5	234.25
40	reading	230.25	234.25					
41								
42								
43								

Figure 6.9 Bar Graph of MAP Growth

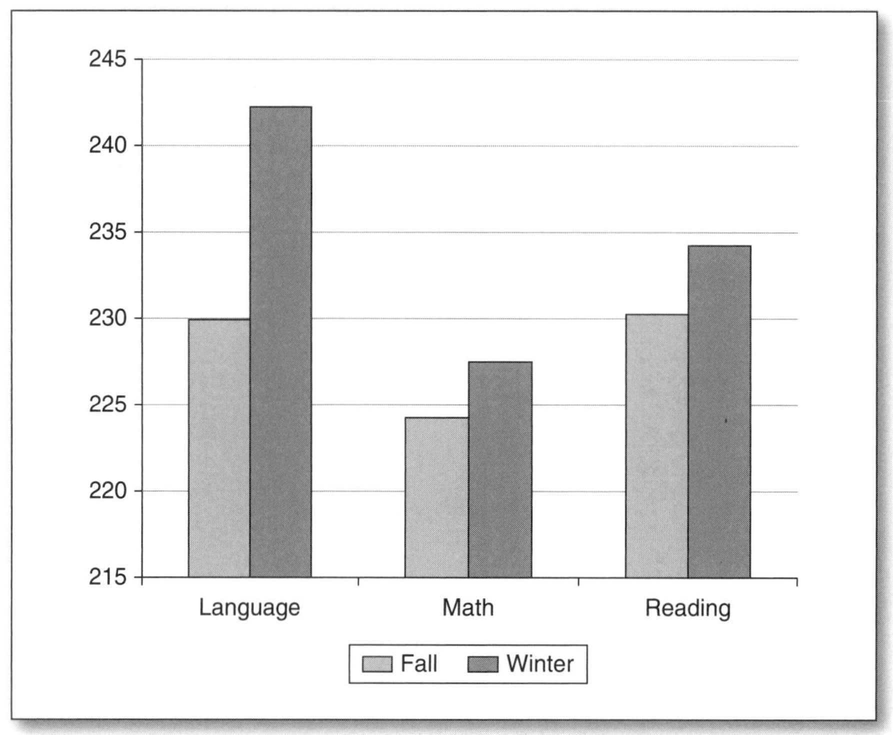

Figure 6.10 Line Graph Visual of MAP Growth

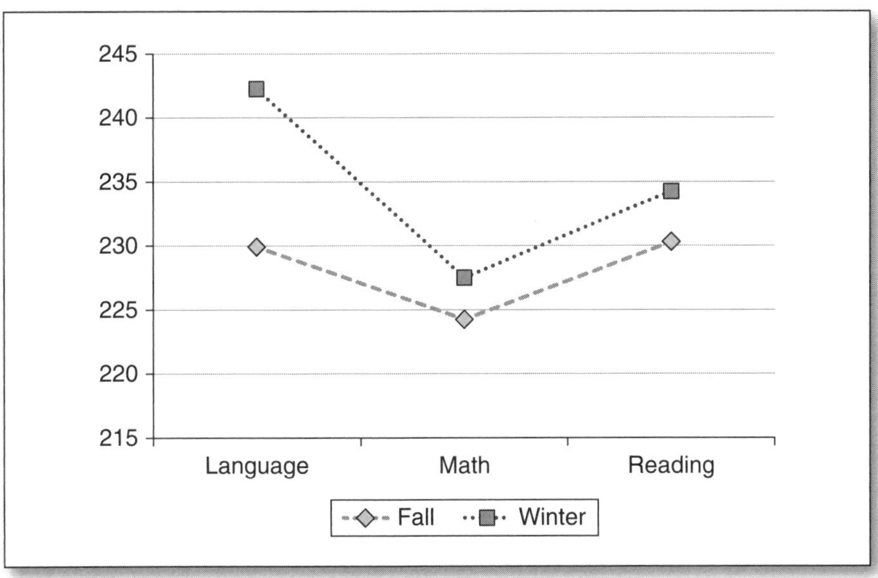

testing periods from fall to winter. We might also disaggregate the data to compare these students to those who received just the SSS classroom intervention or no school counseling interventions at all (even more support for your effectiveness).

Simple visuals can also be created to capture process data. For example, you can use a pie chart to create a visual of how many students received various levels of school counseling interventions (see Figure 6.11).

Figure 6.11 Pie Chart Representation of Number of Students Who Received Services

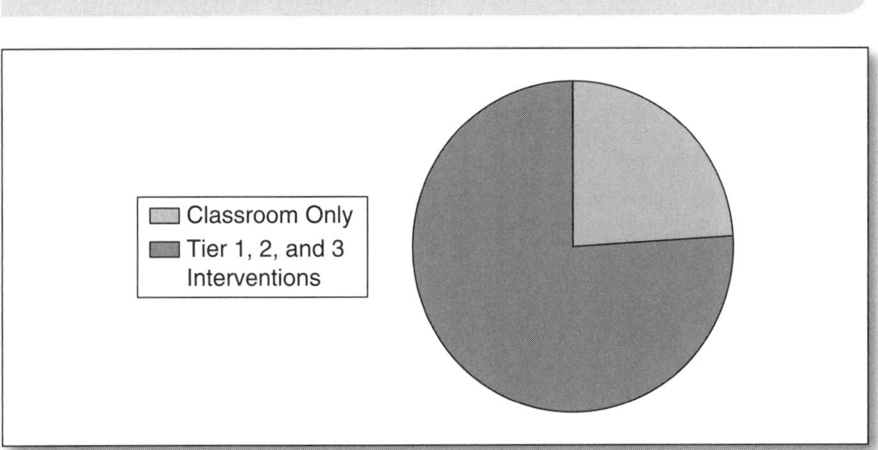

IMPLICATIONS

Now that you have analyzed your data, it's time to determine what the results indicate and what the implications of these findings are for future practice. Noticing trends in the data, considering possible explanations for these trends, and deciding what steps can be taken to improve your data the next time are all suggested (Hatch, 2014). Were you able to accomplish the goals you set? Did your students make the gains you anticipated? If they did, that's fantastic! The interventions you implemented were effective at removing barriers to learning and providing your students with the support they needed to achieve. You can now move on to sharing these success stories with your stakeholders (see Chapter 7) and focusing on your next school counseling goal. If your results did not indicate effectiveness, it's your job to determine why not and what went wrong. For example, did you set your goals too high? Did the intervention you selected not necessarily align with the students' needs? Recall that our goal was to see students make at least 10% more than normal growth (2.2 point gain) on their math MAP scores from fall to winter after receiving the SSS small-group intervention. Figure 6.12 shows the grade-level growth for MAP RIT scores for both fall and winter in math. The full document reflecting expected MAP growth can be retrieved at schools.cms.k12.nc.us/eastoverES/Documents/ACPS-MAP%20Parent%20Brochure.pdf. Our sample for analysis was looking at differences in these scores among students in the eighth grade. Notice that the average gains made from fall to winter for students in the eighth grade who are "below grade level" are only a few points (anywhere from one to about three). Our goal was for our intervention group to gain 2.2 points. However, going back to our sample, we can see that students who received our intervention made average gains of approximately six points. How encouraging!

A final analysis will be conducted in order to compare the growth of students who only received classroom guidance intervention to those who received Tier 2 and 3 small-group and individual counseling supports as well. Fortunately, we have already collected and coded our data by the varying intervention levels (1 = classroom guidance only, 2 = classroom guidance and small group, 3 = classroom guidance and individual counseling, and 4 = classroom guidance, small group, and individual counseling). Running a comparative analysis that distinguishes these subgroups of students can provide another level of information about the value of your services. Refer back to Figure 6.4, and note that this information is listed in the intervention column and corresponding key. From your original data set, simply do another sort by the intervention column, and copy and paste the various groups ONLY into a separate spreadsheet. Figure 6.13, on page 98, shows a screenshot of the copy-and-pasted information for students coded

Figure 6.12 Grade Level Growth for MAP RIT Scores

Eighth-grade average scores for students scoring "below grade level"

Fall MAP *Math* RIT Score

Grade	Above Grade Level	At Grade Level	Below Grade Level	1-Grade Below	2-Grades Below
1	165+	164	149-163	148-	
2	180+	179	165-178	149-164	148-
3	193+	192	180-191	165-179	164-
4	204+	203	193-202	180-192	179-
5	213+	212	204-211	193-203	192-
6	220+	219	213-218	204-212	203-
7	226+	225	220-224	213-219	212-
8	231+	230	226-229	220-225	219-
9	234+	233	231-232	226-230	225-

Eighth-grade average scores for students scoring "below grade level"

Winter MAP *Math* RIT Score

Grade	Above Grade Level	At Grade Level	Below Grade Level	1-Grade Below	2-Grades Below
1	172+	171	153-170	152-	
2	187+	186	172-185	153-171	152-
3	200+	199	187-198	172-186	171-
4	209+	208	200-207	187-199	186-
5	217+	216	209-215	200-208	199-
6	223+	222	217-221	209-216	208-
7	229+	228	223-227	217-222	216-
8	233+	232	229-231	223-228	222-
9	235+	234	233	229-232	228-

as 2s, 3s, or 4s, meaning they received small-group and/or individual counseling in addition to classroom guidance.

Next, follow the same process of copying and pasting the information for students coded as 1s who only received the classroom intervention, and run those averages. Figure 6.14, on the next page, reflects this information for our sample data set. Finally, copy and paste the analyzed information comparing fall scores and winter scores by group. This information is shown in Figure 6.15.

Your final step is to copy the information in the grid, and then select the Charts option in the Options menu, and create a visual representation for each. (We have selected a line graph to depict group differences and growth over time). Figures 6.16, 6.17, and 6.18 reflect the information from the grid above in visual forms. From these visuals, note that our targeted group—those students who were identified for services because they had previously scored novice or apprentice on MAP—appears to make consistent gains from the fall to winter testing periods. Even more exciting is that our Tier 2 and Tier 3 interventions are proving effective at closing the achievement gap in reading!

Figure 6.13 Screenshot of Data Set Sorted and Analyzed for Students Who Received Additional Tier 2 and/or Tier 3 Counseling Services

C	D	E	F	G	H	I
Intervention	Map Scores-Language (Fall)	Map Scores-Math (Fall)	Map Scores-Reading (Fall)	Map Scores-Language (Winter)	Map Scores-Math (Winter)	Map Scores-Reading (Winter)
4	224	227	222	230	233	230
4	223	228	237	229	237	242
4	232	235	230	241	239	234
4	230	219	222	238	220	222
3	232	219	233	235	222	236
3	247	224	236	255	229	245
2	239	239	230	248	243	234
2	229	240	244	235	243	248
2	232	228	235	233	236	239
2	220	240	222	227	244	226
2	230	243	236	239	247	239
2	228	235	244	238	244	248
2	229	228	240	230	234	245
2	238	243	243	245	250	245
2	230	236	239	235	245	249
2	226	231	237	229	239	240
2	229	236	225	238	243	226
2	229	229	237	235	234	242
18 students	230.388889	232.222222	234	236.666667	237.888889	238.333333

Figure 6.14 Screenshot of Data Set Sorted and Analyzed for Students Who Received Only Tier 1 Counseling Services

Intervention	Map Scores-Language (Fall)	Map Scores-Math (Fall)	Map Scores-Reading (Fall)	Map Scores-Language (Winter)	Map Scores-Math (Winter)	Map Scores-Reading (Winter)
1	230	235	231	234	240	239
1	245	249	241	250	252	249
1	243	245	243	246	248	252
1	242	236	242	247	242	248
1	243	243	250	243	253	256
1	247	239	242	249	247	243
6 students	241.666667	241.166667	241.5	244.833333	247	247.833333

Figure 6.15 Grid of Analyzed Scores for Fall and Winter by Group

	Language F	Language V	Math Fall	Math Wint	Reading Fal	Reading Winter
Tier 1 Only	241.67	244.83	241.16	247	241.5	247.83
Tier 1 & Tie	229.92	236	235.67	241.83	236	247.08

Figure 6.16 Line Graph Representation of Analyzed MAP Language Scores From Fall 2014 to Winter 2015 by Group

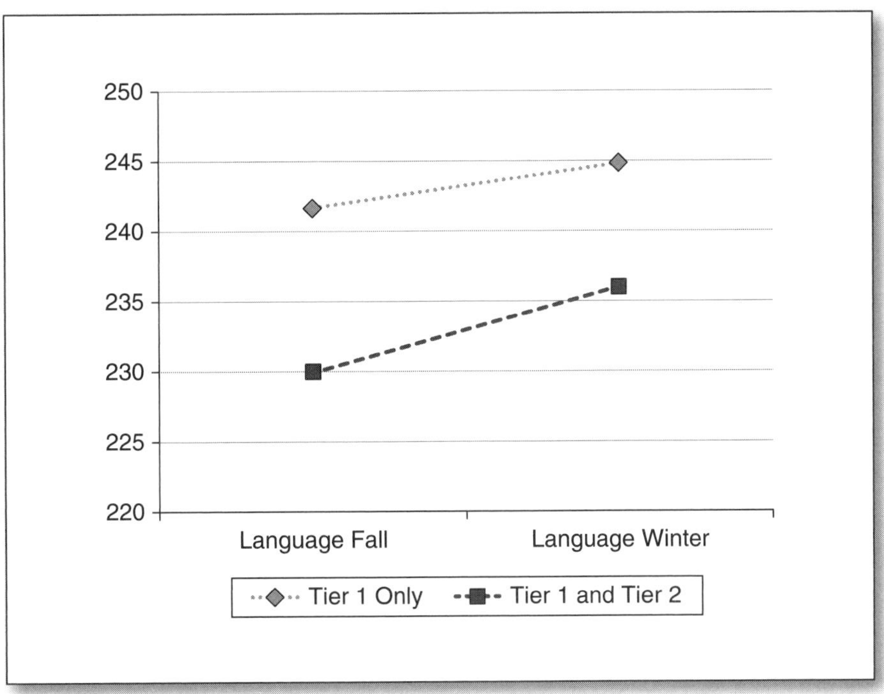

Figure 6.17 Line Graph Representation of Analyzed MAP Math Scores From Fall 2014 to Winter 2015 by Group

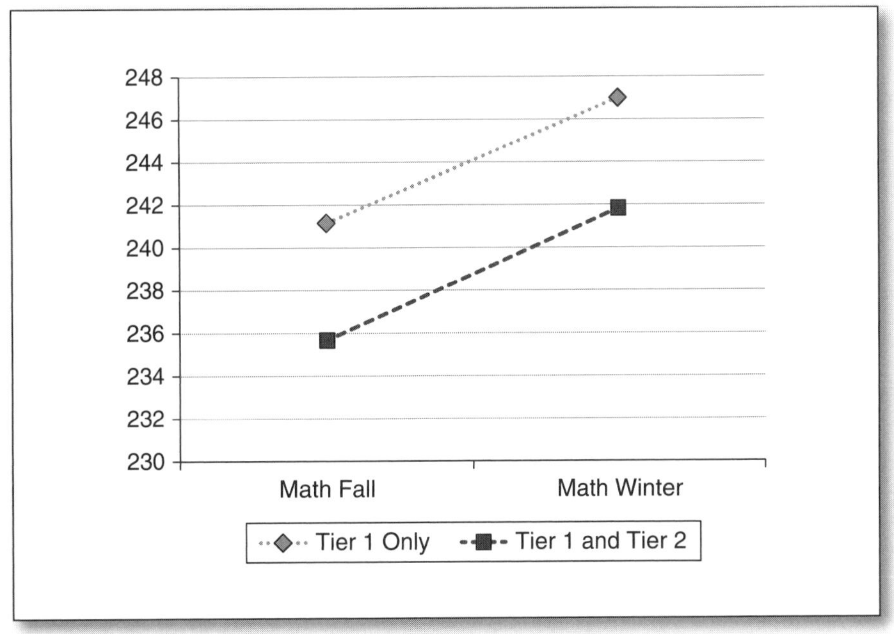

Figure 6.18 Line Graph Representation of Analyzed MAP Reading Scores From Fall 2014 to Winter 2015 by Group

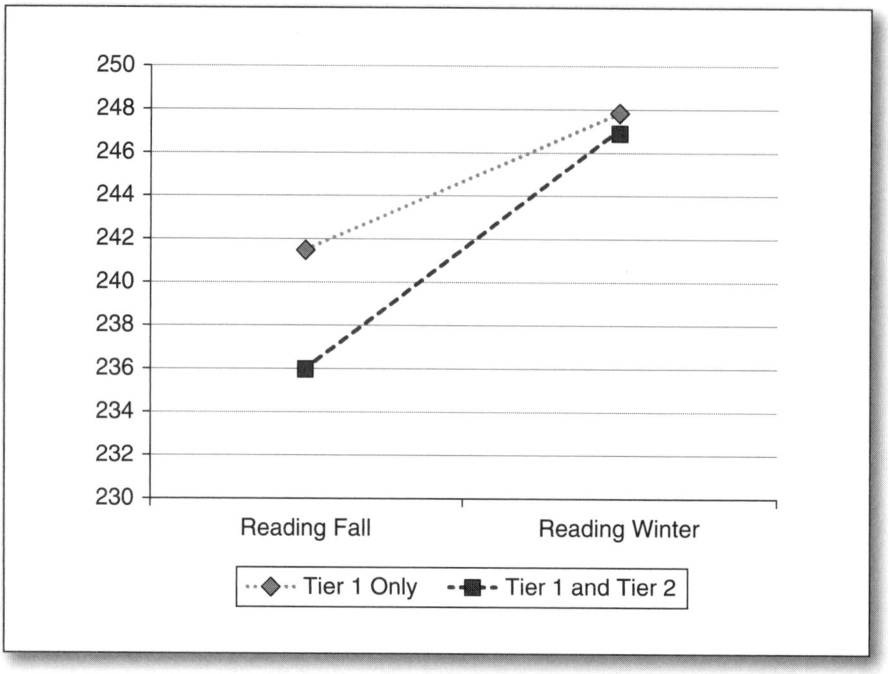

250
248
246
244
242
240
238
236
234
232
230
Reading Fall
Reading Winter
Tier 1 Only
Tier 1 and Tier 2

A COMPLETE LOGIC MODEL

This chapter has contained many useful strategies for evaluating school counseling interventions using Excel. You may find that there are other people at your school, at your central office, or in your community who are willing to help with the data analysis if you have your data organized using an Excel document. It may be helpful to gather your data using the Excel document and illustrate why you were gathering that data using your logic model. For example, you might take both the logic model and the Excel document to the people helping you and use the two visuals to explain your data-driven process, how you matched the needs of your students with your interventions, and what you were hoping to evaluate. In our experience, school counselors who reach out for help locally, regionally, or nationally through listservs such as ASCA Scene (http://scene.schoolcounselor.org/home) receive assistance. However, it will be difficult for others to help you if you have not organized your data well using an Excel spreadsheet or if you are not able to explain your process using a logic model (see Figure 6.19).

Figure 6.19 Logic Model: Completed

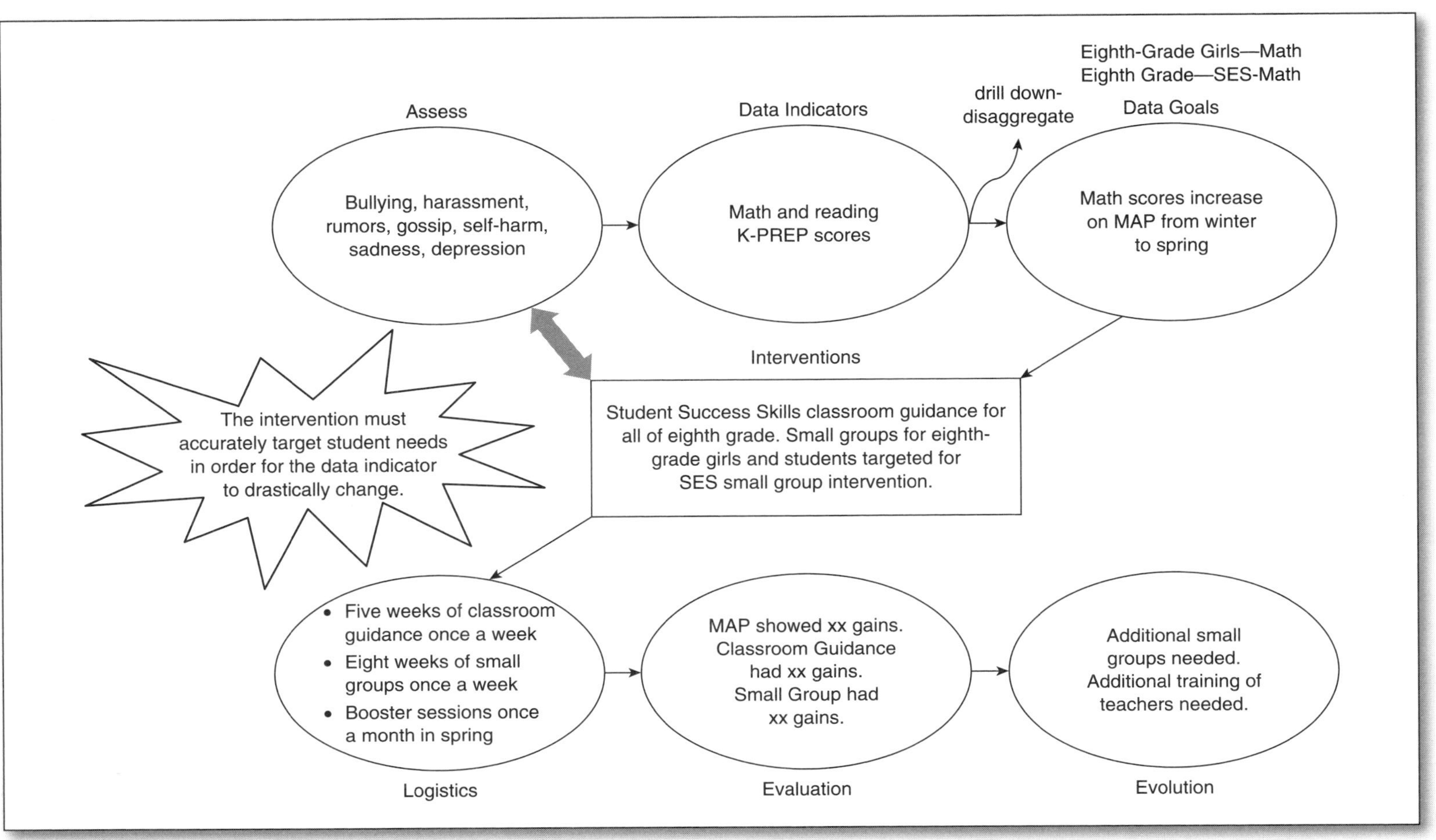

Source: Adapted from Dimmitt, Carey, & Hatch (2007).

FULFILLING COMPONENTS OF RAMP

Thus far, the data-driven comprehensive school counseling process has resulted in multiple components of the Recognized ASCA Model Program (RAMP) being fulfilled. In previous chapters, beliefs, missions, and visions were created to direct the school counseling program. School counseling goals were evolved to serve as the driving force of the school counseling program. The skills gained in the evaluation process apply directly to informing RAMP components eight, nine, ten, and eleven. These four components require school counselors to use American School Counselor Association templates to describe a curriculum action plan (Item 8), the results of implementing that curriculum (Item 9), a counseling small-group intervention and its results (Item 10), and a closing-the-gap intervention and its results (Item 11).

To successfully plan a whole-grade or whole-school curriculum action plan, it is necessary to have an evaluation plan as well. The results of the intervention must be reported to ASCA to earn RAMP recognition. Further, as detailed in this chapter, small-group interventions targeting equity gaps may be used to meet the requirements of both the small-group results report (Item 10) and the closing-the-gap results report (Item 11). The ASCA recommends you plan different interventions to use within these items; attempt to avoid using one small-group intervention to fulfill the requirements of both Items 10 and 11. It is also vital that school counselors discuss the evolution and changes to be made to curriculum interventions and small-group interventions from one year to the next. These evolutions and changes need to be, in part, driven by the results of the analysis. The process described in this chapter will help drive the narrative about what changes need to be made in the interventions to increase their effectiveness.

The previous two chapters would also be helpful to create concrete intervention planning and evaluation strategies for school counseling goals. These details would be helpful to include in the annual agreement (Item 5). Further, one weakness of school counselors we often observe is a lack of a master calendar. Calendars are an organizational best practice that school counselors can post digitally or physically outside an office to provide educational stakeholders with insight into how time is spent to impact student growth and achievement. Use master calendars (Item 7) as another way to harness momentum and support from others at the school and in the surrounding community. Your goal, intervention, and evaluation planning should all be represented within the master calendar.

7 Disseminating Results and Sustaining the Program

A Checklist for Disseminating Results and Sustaining the Program	
Completed?	**Processes (including any necessary materials)**
❒	Ensure your visuals effectively communicate your results.
❒	Create a Flashlight PowerPoint to communicate your results.
❒	Practice communicating the impact of your interventions.
❒	Disseminate your Flashlights through newsletters, on the school website, at parent meetings, at administrative meetings, and at school board meetings.
❒	Consider presenting your results at local, state, or regional conferences.
❒	Add components of your school counseling program into your school's improvement plan.

PURPOSE OF SUSTAINING THE PROGRAM

At the most recent national Evidence-Based School Counseling Conference (http://coehs.nku.edu/centers/nkcee/center_at_work/profdevinitiatives/EBSCConference.html), a superintendent, Steve Hutton (2015), gave a presentation titled "Sustainability: The Missing Piece for Long-Term Success." Hutton's presentation highlighted the dangers of adopting new content without paying attention to the systemic culture change, to systemic reinforcement of fidelity, and to maintaining the intervention over time. Hutton proposed five guiding questions (http://coehs.nku.edu/content/dam/coehs/docs/cfee/Sustainability%20Presentation%20_Steve%20Hutton.pdf) to direct the sustainability of any program:

1. Where are we now?
2. Where do we want to go?
3. How will we get there?
4. How will we know when we are there?
5. How will we keep the momentum going?

Hutton reinforced the idea that even when implementing an outstanding evidence-based intervention, if one implements it poorly, without fidelity, and with no eye toward maintenance, it is doomed to failure. An amazing, highly evidence-based intervention poorly implemented is still a poor intervention. Intentionally following the process outlined in this book takes discipline. It takes a focus on changing systems, changing school culture, creating a common vision, creating a common language, and reinforcing what works so that all stakeholders support the sustainability of the initiative.

Using the processes and visuals presented in this book, we should be able to clearly articulate where we are now after we have assessed the situation, defined the needs of our students, solidified our goals, chosen interventions, and implemented evaluation strategies (see Figure 7.1). At the conclusion of this process, we will have results to disseminate and evaluation to undertake. The evaluation process will clearly define "where we want to go" in our next steps: what is working, what needs to be tweaked, what needs to be replaced, and why things were successful or unsuccessful (usually a result of a poor match between needs and intervention or a lack of implementation with fidelity).

Notice also that our process clearly provides us with evidence of "how we got there," due to the match between interventions and student needs.

Figure 7.1 Process for Building Evidence-Based School Counseling Program

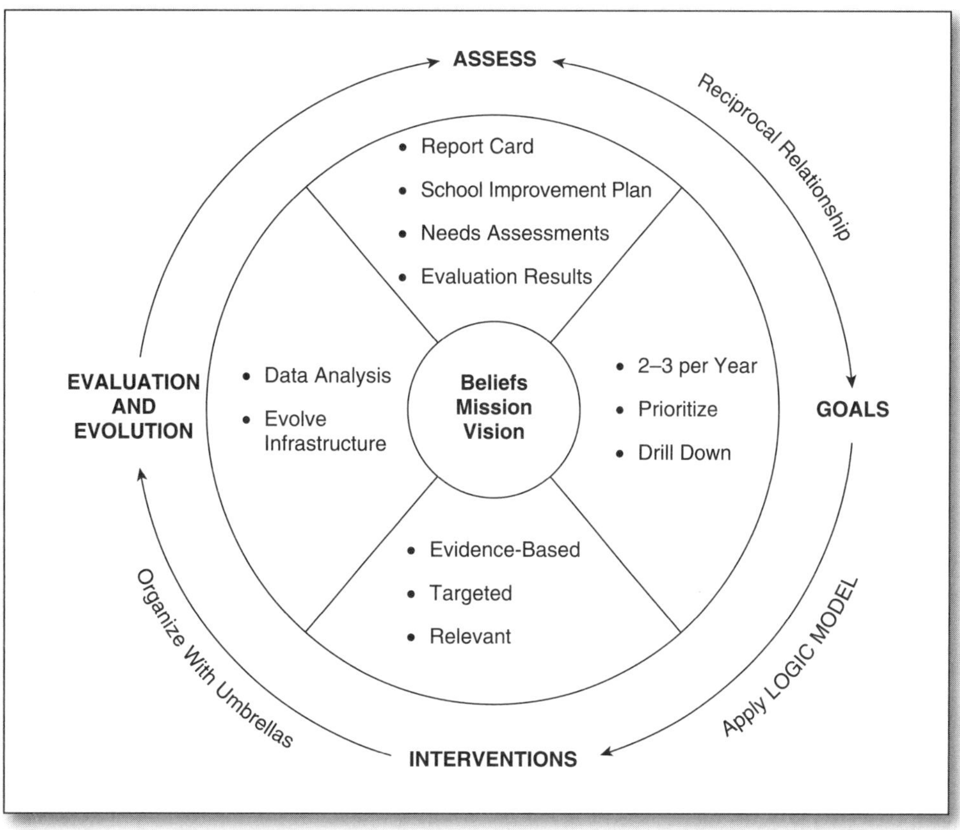

Note: The arrows indicate the reciprocal relationship of various aspects of the process.

We will also "know when we are there" because students' needs will be addressed, barriers to their success will be removed, and the culture of their success is usually contagious and celebrated by the teachers, school counselors, administrators, and other educational stakeholders involved in supporting their success. The last question remains, "How will we keep the momentum going?"

Notice that the steps of the visual representing the data-driven comprehensive school counseling process align with the steps within our logic model (see Figure 7.2). A logic model is helpful to apply the steps as we determine the red flags represented by equity gaps, dig deeper to assess what the true issue is, and carefully choose interventions to meet the needs of our students. As we follow the flow of the logic model, we are also fulfilling steps within the data-driven comprehensive school counseling process. Many school counselors find it is useful to print out multiple blank logic

Figure 7.2 A Completed Logic Model

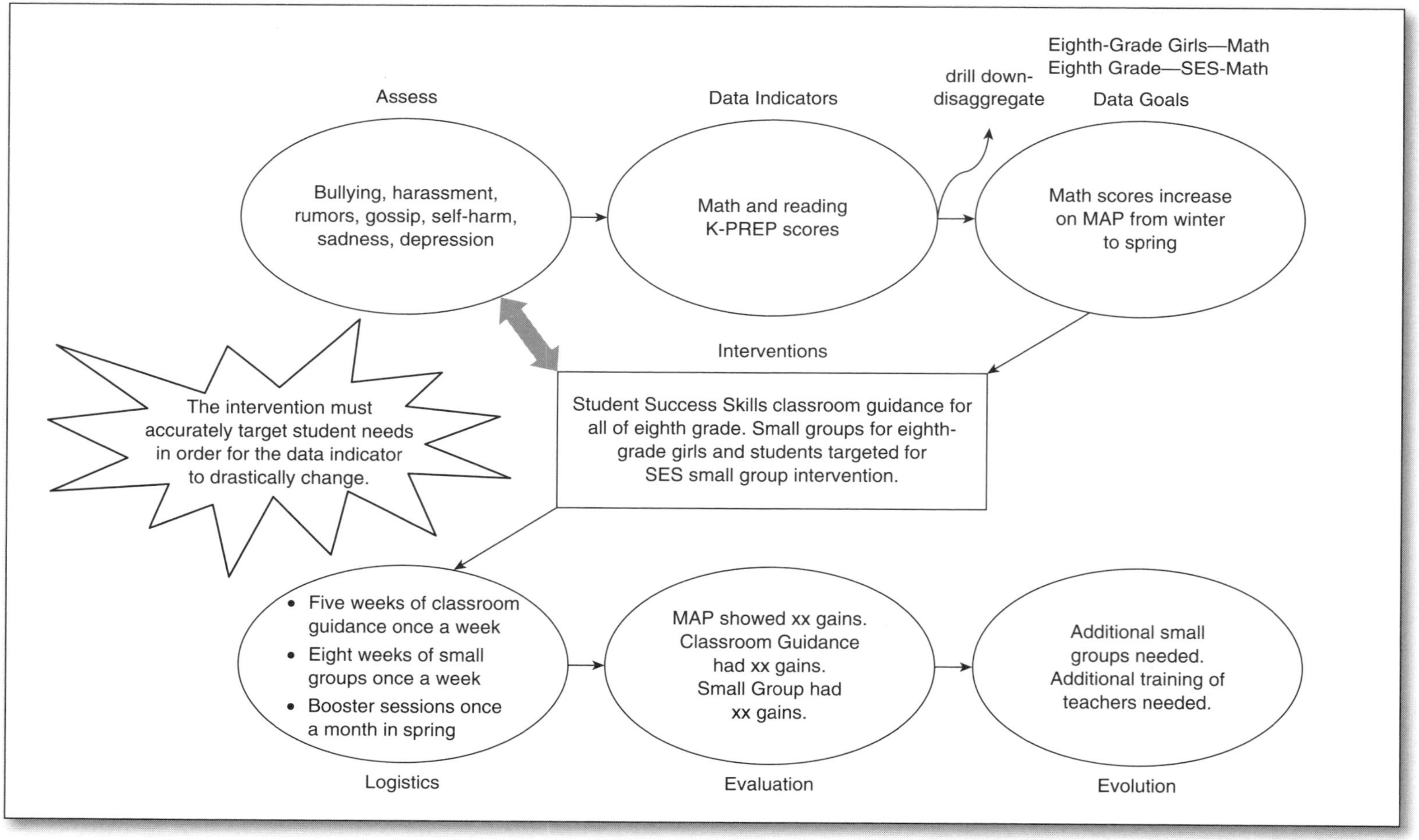

Assess

Bullying, harassment, rumors, gossip, self-harm, sadness, depression

Data Indicators

Math and reading K-PREP scores

drill down-disaggregate

Eighth-Grade Girls—Math
Eighth Grade—SES-Math

Data Goals

Math scores increase on MAP from winter to spring

The intervention must accurately target student needs in order for the data indicator to drastically change.

Interventions

Student Success Skills classroom guidance for all of eighth grade. Small groups for eighth-grade girls and students targeted for SES small group intervention.

- Five weeks of classroom guidance once a week
- Eight weeks of small groups once a week
- Booster sessions once a month in spring

Logistics

MAP showed xx gains. Classroom Guidance had xx gains. Small Group had xx gains.

Evaluation

Additional small groups needed. Additional training of teachers needed.

Evolution

Source: Adapted from Dimmitt, Carey, & Hatch (2007).

models (see the online resource center at http://www.corwin.com/ZyromskiEvidenceBased) to use as they plan various school counseling program goals each year. As you continue to build goals and track school counseling interventions, using a goal-tracking sheet is vital to both track goals and share the progress of the program with administrators. We call the planning tool we use the "School Counseling Program Goal-Tracking Form" (see online resource center), and it was created by Pendleton County school counselors. It aligns well with tracking sheets offered by other authors and the ASCA.

One of the dangers in not prioritizing each step of the data-driven comprehensive school counseling process detailed above is that school leaders change often. It is quite common for principals to move schools, move to central office, retire, or shift positions for some other reason. As leadership shifts, the culture that was created could easily be undermined internally. Without the data to illustrate the value of the school counseling program, the priorities of the administration can move quickly, sometimes catching school counselors by surprise. Often school counselors have the "nice counselor" mentality, simply out of fear of repercussion, a loss of respect, or a loss of appreciation. In response, some school counselors say yes to everything, which results in an inability to prioritize the interventions that directly impact student achievement. Having gained a place of status, respect, and freedom under one administration, that status can shift and be lost quickly under the subsequent administration. Without data to illustrate the value of school counseling interventions, the prioritization of those interventions within the school culture is lost, and the job of school counselors is marginalized to clerical quasiadministrator without any direct impact on student success.

Sadly, this has been the experience of some colleagues of ours, who one year considered themselves the most fortunate school counselors in the world with the ability to do their jobs the way they dreamed and the next year found themselves searching for a job. Administration changed, and without results data to illustrate their worth, these school counselors were quickly marginalized within the system. In his presentation, Hutton suggested six important steps to ensure sustainability, which included the following:

1. Keeping the priorities the priorities—don't let your eye wander from the most important interventions you are implementing.
2. Ensure you continue to monitor the fidelity of your interventions and collect data regarding outcomes continuously.
3. Build a data system that provides regular updates that are easy to manage and relevant to the school's goals.

4. Strive to create systems that are efficient and economical, so you are not spending all your time in maintenance and data-crunching roles.

5. Whenever possible, choose evidence-based practices.

6. Celebrate your successes and improvements along the way.

As you follow these six steps, it will be difficult to be pushed out of the system or be moved to the side as the impact of your school counseling program will be celebrated by all educational stakeholders.

TIPS AND TRICKS

It is important to note that it takes three to five years to fully implement a systemic approach to data-driven comprehensive school counseling that is embedded and sustainable. Be patient, be gentle with yourself, and be persistent!

ADVERTISING AND DISSEMINATING INFORMATION

Few school counselors are adept at self-promotion. Fortunately, advocating for our school counseling programs is not self-promotion; it is promotion of how to help our students be successful in life. If we return to the evidence we have about the four constructs students need to be successful in life, as proposed by Squier, Nailor, and Carey (2014), it is clear that often our schools are not helping students increase their motivation, enhance their self-direction, increase their self-knowledge, or learn how to build positive, healthy, and beneficial relationships. School counselors are in the ideal position to equip students with those skills and abilities. When we advocate for our school counseling program, we are advocating for the success of our students.

Not all school counselors have been taught how to advocate. The best school counselor education programs around the country ensure their students engage in advocacy projects while completing their master's degrees in school counseling. However, not all school counselor education programs equip their graduates with the skills to advocate. Fortunately, most school counselors are lifelong learners who possess the motivation, self-direction, and self-knowledge to be successful in life. School counselors' unique ability to build strong relationships not only helps in their everyday work but is vital in advocacy efforts. One way to think about advocacy is to consider how to best build relationships with educational stakeholders who make important decisions about how to best help students. How do we best build relationships with teachers, administration, parents, district personnel, school board members, regional educational leaders, state educational and political leaders, and national leaders?

It is the premise of the authors that disseminating the impact school counselors have on student achievement is a natural way to gain traction in our schools, our communities, and the educational profession. We began the book providing a research base establishing evidence of school counselors' impact on student achievement. How many school counselors use that research to advocate for increased roles in their schools? How many school counselors share how two economists (Carrell & Hoekstra, 2011) suggested that having a school counselor has a similar impact on student achievement as increasing the quality of every teacher in the school a significant amount and is twice as effective as reducing class sizes? How many of our administrators know that fact? Imagine telling a central office that hiring a school counselor is more cost-efficient for increasing student achievement than hiring an additional ten teachers in a school of 500 students and showing them the research to back it up (Carrel & Hoekstra, 2011). Plus, according to Carrel and Hoekstra (2011), the presence of a school counselor reduces misbehavior of males by roughly 20% and females by roughly 29%. Hopefully, someone would listen and take notice. They might take more notice, however, if you share your own data about how your school counseling program has impacted your students.

FLASHLIGHTS: TRISH HATCH

It was also mentioned in the preface to this book and in Chapter 1 that the ideas we express are not original but rather collected together from a variety of sources and enhanced with frontlines work with professional school counselors. One great resource from which school counselors can pull pre-post tests, surveys, and other useful tools is Dr. Trish Hatch's website, Hatching Results (http://hatchingresults.com). The components laid out on her website build from other foundational work of hers with Dimmitt and Carey (Dimmitt, Carey, & Hatch, 2007) as well as work by Stone and Dahir (2010) and others. As noted in previous chapters, many resources are available online through various organizations. However, as we have worked with school counselors around the country, we have noticed that Hatch's Flashlight (Hatch, 2014) is easily understood and applied to organize school counseling interventions into visual presentations to disseminate to stakeholders. As a result, we will use that format in this chapter to organize and disseminate results of our school counseling interventions.

Hatch (2014) suggests that the Flashlight shine a light on one thing the school counselor has done to show the results of an intervention or program component. The summary of the Flashlight Approach detailed here is not as exhaustive as Hatch's approach. For those interested in a complete review, please refer to her book. For our purposes, we will present what we consider the imperative components of the Flashlight (see Howell Flashlight Presentation for an example). Although inspired by Hatch's (2014) Flashlight Approach, any errors or omissions are ours. The Flashlight contains a title slide with the name of the presentation, the school, and the school counselor's name(s). Following the title slide, additional slides contain the following components:

a. ASCA Mind-sets and Behaviors addressed by the intervention

b. The data and the need addressed by the school data

c. Relevant research connecting the need to the intervention

d. Process data of the intervention—who, what, when, and how often was the activity conducted?

e. Graphic representations of the pre-post perception data results

f. Results data is related graphically and linked to perception data and targeted goals of the intervention

g. A slide summarizing main points and implications of lessons learned

h. A next-steps slide, which may include limitations, improvements, or subsequent plans

We have found it incredibly important to choose the visuals carefully that we include in our PowerPoint Flashlights. Not all the visuals created in our last chapter will be appropriate or useful to include in our Flashlight. In fact, we only need a couple visuals to effectively communicate the impact of our intervention with the eighth grade and in our small groups. We have created a succinct Flashlight as an example. Important questions to consider as you build your flashlight are the following:

- Have I clearly illustrated the need and how my intervention meets that need?
- Have I clearly connected our intervention to the data goals of the school and the goal of the school counseling program?
- Have I chosen the most effective visual representation of my results? Would a noneducator, nonteacher, non–school counselor understand my presentation?
- Could I present this to my school board in ten minutes?

If you have considered all these questions and fulfilled all the points required by Hatch (2014) listed above, you have most likely created an effective Flashlight.

OVERVIEW

- Middle school demographics
- What are the issues?
- What did students receive?
- Why are we implementing this intervention?
- Goal
- Process data
- Results and implications
- Next steps

EXAMPLE MIDDLE SCHOOL

- **900 Total Students**
  - 529 Free or reduced lunch (58.7%)
  - 744 White (82.6%)
  - 76 Hispanic/Latino (8%)
  - 44 African American (4.8%)
  - 18 Asian (2%)
  - 18 Multiracial (2%)
  - 438 Male (48.6%)
  - 462 Female (51.4%)

WHAT ARE THE ISSUES?

- Bullying, harassment, rumors, and gossip
- Self-harm
- Mood management – sadness and depression
- Self-esteem

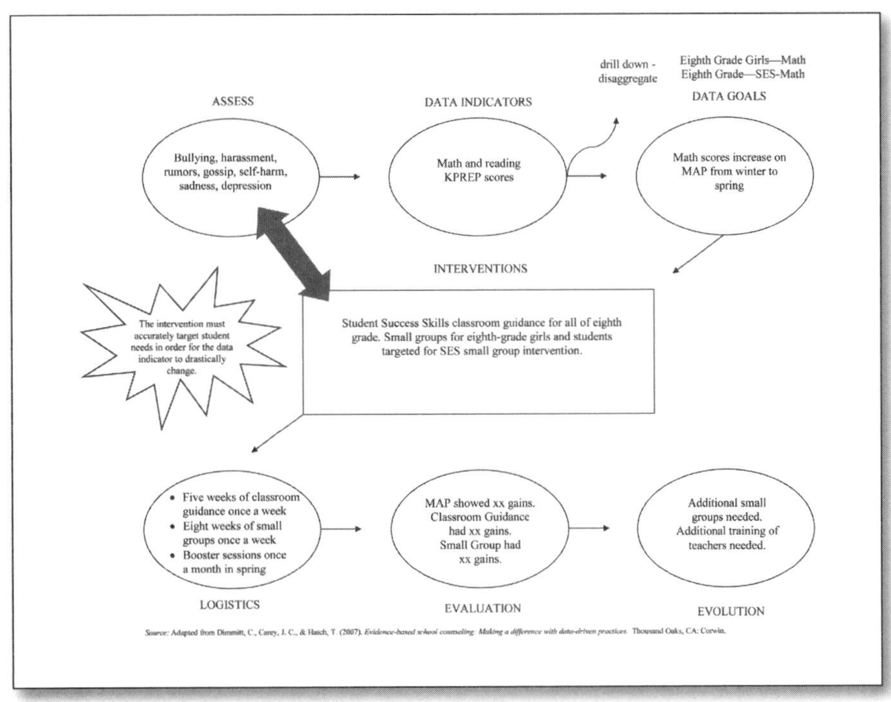

WHAT DID STUDENTS RECEIVE?

- **Students received Student Success Skills**
  - Classroom guidance
    - School counselor–led lessons focused on helping students develop skills needed to improve performance
  - Small groups

WHY ARE WE IMPLEMENTING STUDENT SUCCESS SKILLS?

- Research
  - In the Brigman and Campbell (2005) study, 240 students (12 students from 20 schools) in fifth and sixth grades participated in SSS.
  - 86% of students improved state testing scores in math by an average of 30 points.
  - 78% of students improved state testing scores in reading by an average of 25 points.
  - 69% of students showed improvement on the behavior ranking scale, with an average improvement of 18 points.
- Implications
  - If a program could improve a student's skills for school success, then this skill development would facilitate development in achievement and behavior.
  - Results show positive correlation between group treatment and improvement in both academic performance and behavior.
  - SSS will enable our middle school to reach program goals. (Increasing student MAP scores)

Making a Difference in Student Achievement and Behavior

OUR GOAL

Eighth-grade girls who scored at novice or apprentice the previous year on KPREP or who scored in the lower 25% on the fall MAP evaluation will be targeted for Tier 2 Student Success Skills small groups and, as a result, will increase their MAP scores on the spring math MAP evaluation by 10% more than peers not receiving the SSS small groups.

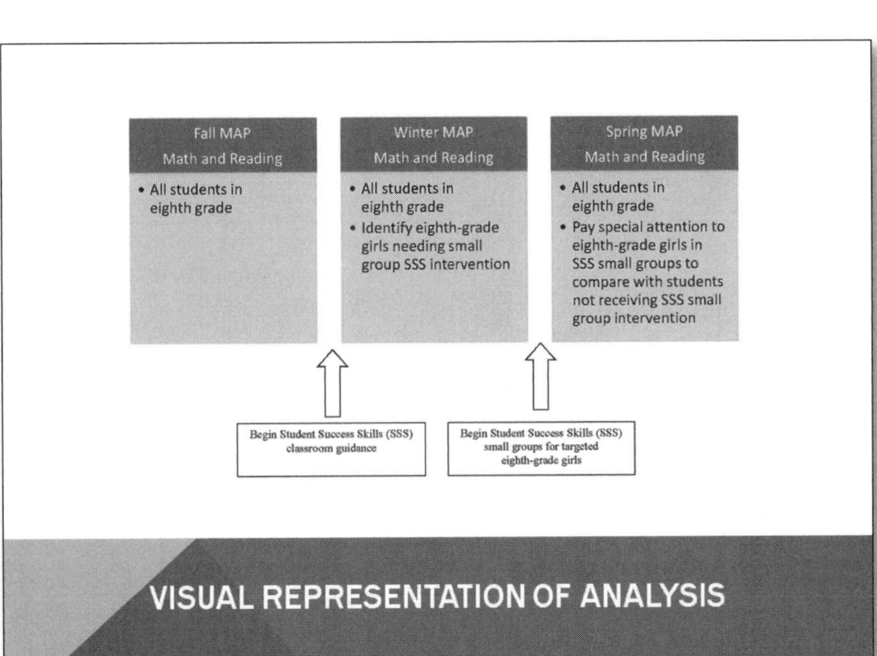
Fall MAP
Math and Reading
• All students in eighth grade
Winter MAP
Math and Reading
• All students in eighth grade
• Identify eighth-grade girls needing small group SSS intervention
Spring MAP
Math and Reading
• All students in eighth grade
• Pay special attention to eighth-grade girls in SSS small groups to compare with students not receiving SSS small group intervention
Begin Student Success Skills (SSS) classroom guidance
Begin Student Success Skills (SSS) small groups for targeted eighth-grade girls
VISUAL REPRESENTATION OF ANALYSIS

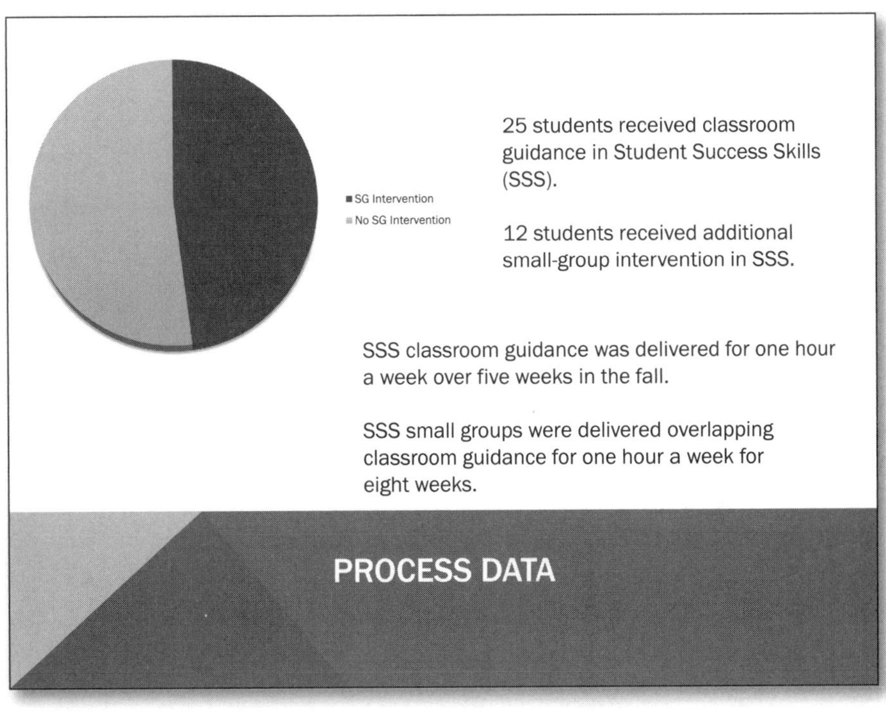
SG Intervention
No SG Intervention
25 students received classroom guidance in Student Success Skills (SSS).
12 students received additional small-group intervention in SSS.
SSS classroom guidance was delivered for one hour a week over five weeks in the fall.
SSS small groups were delivered overlapping classroom guidance for one hour a week for eight weeks.
PROCESS DATA

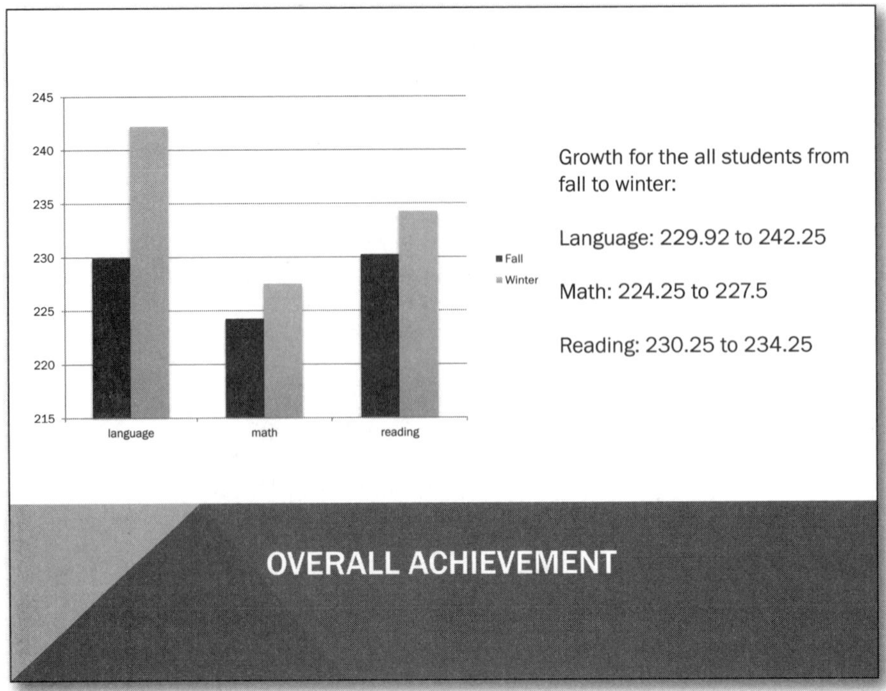
245
240
235
230
225
220
215
language
math
reading
Fall
Winter
Growth for the all students from fall to winter:
Language: 229.92 to 242.25
Math: 224.25 to 227.5
Reading: 230.25 to 234.25
OVERALL ACHIEVEMENT

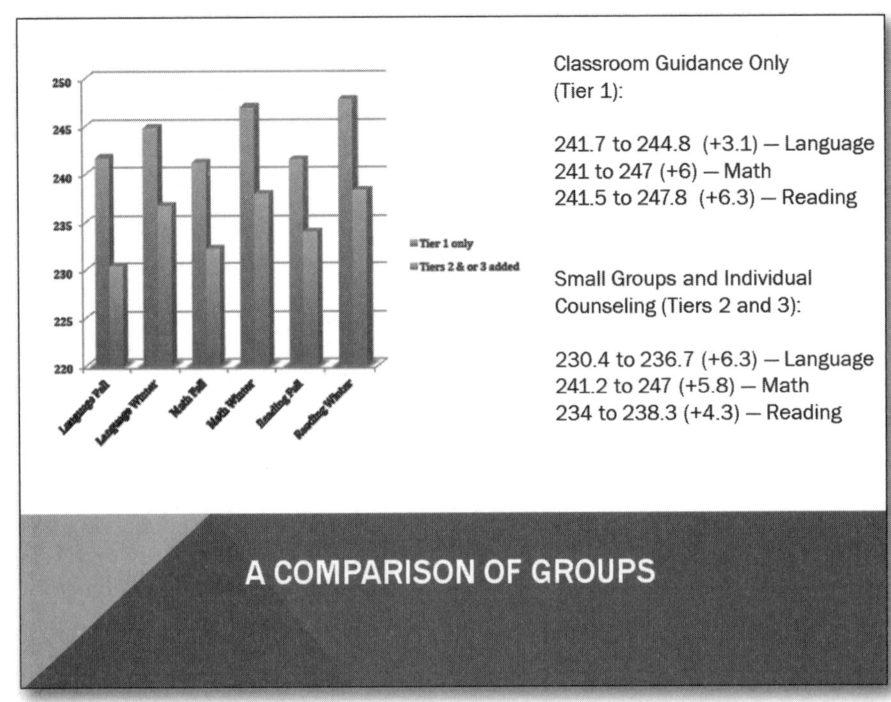
250
245
240
235
230
225
220
Language Fall
Language Winter
Math Fall
Math Winter
Reading Fall
Reading Winter
Tier 1 only
Tiers 2 & or 3 added
Classroom Guidance Only (Tier 1):
241.7 to 244.8 (+3.1) — Language
241 to 247 (+6) — Math
241.5 to 247.8 (+6.3) — Reading
Small Groups and Individual Counseling (Tiers 2 and 3):
230.4 to 236.7 (+6.3) — Language
241.2 to 247 (+5.8) — Math
234 to 238.3 (+4.3) — Reading
A COMPARISON OF GROUPS

The small-group intervention was especially effective in helping close the achievement gap in reading. Our small-group participants gained about three points on the other students (+6.3 compared to +3.1).

However, both groups gained about the same in math (+5.8 compared to +6). This is actually good news as our students tend to struggle and be low achievers in math historically. It will be important to go back and look at our small-group students' scores in math last year to show how a 5.8 point gain is a higher gain than usual for this population.

Finally, in reading, the small group grew at a lower rate than the classroom guidance population (+4.3 compared to +6.3). Exploring the small-group reading increases related to the same students' reading increases on MAP from the previous year will shed more light on if this is a normal growth rate, below normal, or accelerated for these particular students.

ANALYSIS

Next Steps

It seems that our small group was especially effective in Language Arts. However, an analysis of student growth in math and reading through the spring period might prove continued growth in those areas for our gap group as well.

It will be important to return to our students to determine how well their needs are being met. Are they still feeling socially excluded? Do they feel better equipped to handle their sadness and depression? Have they begun making positive friendships at school?

Additional training for teachers to ensure they reinforce the concepts of the SSS curriculum in between lessons will also be important.

Explore implications of why the groups were more impactful for language than math or reading.

Examples of various Flashlights, in addition to the Middle School Example Flashlight, have been included in the online resource center (http://www.corwin.com/ZyromskiEvidenceBased). The Middle School Example Flashlight uses the data and examples from this book. The Flashlights included in the online resource center are samples from school counselors around the country. Again, these Flashlights may not contain all the components of Hatch's Flashlights. To see examples of all components, one can refer to Chapter 11 of her online appendix (http://hatchingresults.com/books/Use-Of-Data/online-appendix.cfm). The point of this exercise in our book is to create a simple visual illustrating the impact of the school counseling intervention on students' success, most often as measured through critical data elements.

Some of our most rewarding moments are when we meet with superintendents to discuss the ramifications of cutting school counselors and have Flashlights to share from schools within the superintendent's own district illustrating the impact their school counselors have on student achievement. Being able to begin the conversation with something like, "Did you know that research by two economists (Carrell & Hoekstra, 2011) suggested that having a school counselor has a similar impact on student achievement as increasing the quality of every teacher in the school a significant amount and is twice as effective as reducing class sizes? They also suggested the presence of a school counselor reduces misbehavior of males by roughly 20% and females by roughly 29%." We then go on to share the data from the six state studies shared in the 2012 special edition of the journal *Professional School Counseling*.

We explain to the superintendent that currently, she has lower student-to-school-counselor ratios than if she releases that school counselor or does not fill a retired school counselor's position. Lower ratios are important, as they result in improved attendance rates (Carey, Harrington, Martin, & Hoffman, 2012; Carey, Harrington, Martin, & Stevenson, 2012), improved attendance rates in high-poverty schools (Lapan, Gysbers, Stanley, & Pierce, 2012), fewer discipline issues (Carey, Harrington, Martin, & Stevenson, 2012; Lapan, Gysbers, et al., 2012), lower suspension rates (Lapan, Whitcomb, & Aleman, 2012), increased rates of attaining technical proficiency in career and vocational programs (Carey, Harrington, Martin, & Hoffman, 2012), and improved completion and graduation rates (Carey, Harrington, Martin, & Hoffman, 2012; Lapan, Gysbers, et al., 2012).

Further, we share that we have been working with their school counseling program and that these programs are built upon the American School Counselor Association's National Model, providing developmental programming for all students in the areas of academic, social/emotional, and career domains. Furthermore, these programs provide differentiated delivery systems. Research (Carey, Harrington, Martin & Stevenson, 2012) suggests that schools that do these two things evidence increased ACT scores, an increased percentage of students taking the ACT, and enhanced student achievement in math and reading, not to mention decreased suspension rates, decreased discipline rates, and increased attendance rates (Carey, Harrington, Martin, & Hoffman, 2012).

In fact, we continue to share with these leaders that we've seen their school counseling programs use data to identify specific needs of students to ensure evidence-based school counseling interventions are selected that meet those student needs. As a result, their school counselors are ensuring that students are increasing their motivation, improving their self-knowledge, enhancing their self-direction, and building strong, positive relationships. Not only have those four constructs been shown to positively impact students' future success (Squier, Nailor, & Carey, 2014), but we actually have examples from your school counselors supporting how their interventions have correlated with increased achievement in math and reading. We may also share additional data illustrating the impact the school counselors have on other data elements, such as post-secondary matriculation rates and increased scholarships and financial aid gained by recent graduates. We have also illustrated how school counselors can improve school culture through Tier 1 and Tier 2 interventions, often resulting in decreased office referrals and increased attendance. Our conversations tend to hone in on areas of focus identified by the superintendent to drive home the impact and relevance of the school counselors.

We then share Flashlights from their own school counselors with the superintendents. Most superintendents want what is best for their students' success. The pressure from the states is tremendous. The pressure to show data outcomes is tremendous. When we create a package that illustrates how students are helped and it results in changes in critical data elements, it relieves some pressure for the superintendent. We have yet to find a superintendent who has not been thrilled with the impacts illustrated through Flashlights. At times, these conversations have resulted in the saving of school counseling positions. In some districts, the financial priorities have even shifted, resulting in additional school counselors being added.

Our hope is that all of us work to see the impact of how our advocacy can help the students in our school buildings but also the students throughout our districts, our regions, our states, and the country. Too often, we find school counselors who feel that since everything is going well within their "kingdom" (their own school building), effort is not needed to advocate for the profession as a whole. The reality is, though, that there are students suffering in neighborhoods all over this country, no matter where we live. If we entered this profession believing that school counseling makes a difference in students' lives, then we have a responsibility to advocate for increased access and opportunity for all students to school counseling services. Whether the student attends my school, the school across town, or the school across the country, that student deserves the opportunity to receive help from a professional school counselor. So we implore you: Share what you are doing and how it makes an impact on student achievement and find your own voice in order to help more students.

ADDING COMPONENTS INTO THE SCHOOL IMPROVEMENT PLAN

One important way to be recognized as an integral part of the school is to ensure that some of the school counseling interventions are listed within the official school improvement plan. School improvement plans are required reports for most schools across our country. School improvement plans (SIPs) are aligned with district improvement plans (DIPs), which are then reported to the state department of education each year. DIPs and SIPs are ways that the state holds the district and school accountable for achieving their goals. In Chapter 2, we used the SIP to understand the focus and goals of the school. Most often, a school improvement plan will focus on academic achievement (as measured by math and reading scores), improvement in school culture, and some sort of professional development. More often than not, a focus on achievement will appear in every SIP, though the school culture and professional development may vary by school. The important point to remember is that the state department of education is reading these reports to determine what the district and school values and prioritizes to achieve their goals and make positive impacts on student achievement.

Fortunately, as illustrated throughout this book, school counseling interventions impact student achievement. Therefore, we need to be inserting school counseling interventions in the academic section of the SIP and the DIP. In the online resource center (http://www.corwin.com/ZyromskiEvidenceBased), we have included multiple examples of DIPs in which school counselors are listed as interventions to achieve district goals. Similarly, in previous chapters, we have included numerous examples of SIPs in which school counseling interventions are listed to achieve SIP goals.

One example of a DIP that has school counseling and school counselors listed throughout the plan is submitted each year by the Erlanger-Elsmere Independent School District. Over the previous five years, the Erlanger-Elsmere Independent School District has moved from half-time school counselors split across elementary schools to having enough school counselors across the district to reach the ASCA recommended ratio of 1:250. Some of the school counselors have been hired through Elementary and Secondary School Counseling Grants. However, more importantly, others have been funded directly by the district. Dr. Kathy Burkhardt believes in the value of data-driven school counselors. Notice in the DIP that school counselors are listed in the achievement goal and are situated on leadership teams with principals and other administrators in charge of supporting students' transitions from one school to another. Evidence-based school counseling interventions are listed within the DIP as are the requirement for school counselors to have needs assessments and Tier 1, Tier 2, and Tier 3 interventions.

School counselors are used throughout the district to help ensure students are reading at grade level (through school counseling interventions, not reading remediation), help support schoolwide positive-behavior support systems, help students transition successfully to and from their alternative schools as needed, and help ensure students graduate from high school and are college and career ready. This district has professional learning communities (PLCs) in which school counselors receive professional development (PD) specific to their needs. This PD is relevant and task-oriented and results in a common definition of professional school counseling across the district as well as within each school.

A natural extension of the emphasis on the integration of school counseling interventions and school counselors throughout the DIP is the same representation within SIP within the district. For example, Lindeman Elementary, one of the elementary schools in Erlanger-Elsmere Independent Schools has school counselors listed as vital components of the SIP. The word *counselor* is listed at least 25 different times related to interventions and tracking. This count is not about the total number of times the word *counselor* is listed, as it is often listed multiple times in one line. Rather, it is about the number of times the word is listed related to a specific program, task, or intervention on the SIP. It is clear from reading the Lindeman SIP that the school counseling program and the school counselors are a valued and integral part of the mission of the school.

Similarly, for the middle school in Erlanger-Elsmere, Tichenor Middle School, the school counseling program is interwoven throughout the SIP. The counseling program and counselors are listed on thirty-four of the strategies and approaches across the school. Often, the term *professional school counselor* is listed. As you can imagine, the school counselors feel valued and part of the core identity of the school when the leadership team includes them, refers to them as *professional school counselors*, and values their interventions on everything from transitions to academics to college and career readiness. For an easy indication of how integrated into the school culture and how valued your school counseling interventions are as they relate to helping students reach school goals, refer to the school improvement plan.

To gain entry to the school improvement plan and district improvement plan, do the following:

a. Download the current DIP and SIP for your school and district.

b. Highlight the goals and current strategies in which you feel you already have programs and interventions in place that make an impact.

c. Prepare your Flashlight presentation to illustrate how your interventions made an impact on the DIP and SIP goals.

d. Ask for a thirty-minute meeting with the administration of your school and central-office administration. Let them know you would like to share data that supports their DIP and SIP.

e. Be sure you bring enough copies of the Flashlight that administrators can leave with a hard copy.

f. Bring an updated version of the DIP and SIP in which you have inserted the school counseling program and interventions. Most often, the DIP and SIP are PDF files. Instead of rewriting the entire DIP or SIP, just create sticky-note comments within the PDF (use the Comments function tab of Adobe PDF). Explain you wanted to save them work while supporting their goals and outcomes by showing how the school counseling program has led to increased goal attainment for the district and school over the previous year. Ask them at the end of the meeting if they would like electronic versions of the documents you handed out and if they would like you to join the committee that updates the DIP and SIP each year.

g. Be sure to keep tracking the data related to the DIP and SIP each year. It is embarrassing to fall behind and not have a report ready that relates to a DIP and SIP.

Once you have gained access to the DIP and SIP, you will notice that you are involved in more administrative meetings than you may have been previously. This is a good sign that you are included as part of the leadership team at the school and valued as a contributor to critical data change. It is important to be at the table during important decision-making regarding prioritizing interventions. Money and support is distributed to priorities. The school counseling program needs to be a priority. One way to support it as a priority is to ensure it is in the district and school improvement plans.

FULFILLING COMPONENTS OF RAMP

It was mentioned in Chapter 1 that evidence-based, data-driven comprehensive school counseling directly addresses eight of the twelve items included in RAMP submissions. The eight components that are addressed through the data-driven comprehensive school counseling process using evidence-based interventions are as follows:

- Vision statement (Item 1)
- Mission statement (Item 2)
- Program goals (Item 3)
- School counseling curriculum action plan (Item 8)
- School counseling curriculum report (Item 9)
- Small-group action plan and results report (Item 10)
- Closing equity gap results report (Item 11)
- Program evaluation report (Item 12)

As mentioned previously, the annual agreement (Item 5) and calendars (Item 7) are valuable tools used to prioritize time and to organize implementation of evidence-based interventions throughout the school year. As shown in previous chapters, if a data-driven comprehensive school counselor simply tracks the evolution of the school counseling program through the cycle (see Figure 7.1), then the school counselor can complete the forms necessary to submit for a Recognized ASCA Model Program (RAMP) designation if one plans accordingly. To plan accordingly, begin at least one year ahead of time (see https://www.schoolcounselor.org/school-counselors-members/ramp/application-process to learn about the process), and ensure your administration is on board with the annual agreement and other documentation needed to keep a record of the impact of your program and interventions. Ensure you use the ASCA RAMP forms as you plan and record your school counseling interventions. Build a strong advisory council, and ask them to help you navigate the process. Thus, if you plan to submit a RAMP application in October 2017 (they are due each October), begin planning, building your advisory council, downloading forms, and creating your annual agreement for the fall 2016–spring 2017 school year. It takes time to get organized and to coordinate support—plan accordingly. You can do it!

CONCLUSIONS

Many school counselors begin the year with the best of intentions regarding collecting data to illustrate the impact of their school counseling program. However, once in the midst of the chaos of the school year, it is extremely difficult to keep track of all the activities and interventions being implemented. Use a time tracker tool to stay organized and to track your time. A free time tracker tool is offered at ezanalyze.com, and many videos are available on the site to teach school counselors how to use the free tool. A few simple steps will increase the chances that you will stay focused on tracking the impact of your school counseling interventions throughout the school year. We have noticed that school counselors who do the following are highly successful at producing meaningful results at the end of the year, representing the impact they had on student success:

a. Plan during the previous spring and summer. Do not wait until the fall to plan out your school counseling goals.

b. Create one school counseling goal and one Excel sheet to track that goal. As mentioned in Point A, create this goal and Excel spreadsheet at the end of the previous year, not at the start of the present school year.

c. Use a logic model to determine the data indicators, drill down to identify a specific population, learn about that population's needs, choose an intervention that meets those needs, and plan logistics and evaluation.

d. Use a goal-tracking sheet (see the online resource center at http://www.corwin.com/ZyromskiEvidenceBased) to plan how to assess the impact of your intervention using perception and results data.

e. Use a master calendar to visually represent when your intervention will take place and with whom.

f. Share your plan with your administration and even have them sign off on the goal as a priority using the ASCA Annual Agreement.

g. Collaborate with other school counselors on building goals to meet periodically to encourage each other and keep each other accountable.

h. No matter the chaos that occurs, be sure to prioritize the intervention involved with your goal. Covet the time needed to deliver this intervention with fidelity to ensure you have the highest chance to make a measurable impact on student success.

i. Collect and organize data at holiday breaks.

j. Ask for help in analyzing your data from people at your central office or local institutes of higher education.

k. Create a Flashlight presentation and choose which visuals to create to represent your outcomes carefully. You want your visuals to clearly and concisely represent the impact of the intervention.

l. Always conclude with next steps and evolutionary steps to improve next time.

Most importantly, know that you can implement a data-driven comprehensive school counseling program. Few school counselors today were originally trained in these strategies, yet hundreds are successfully leading goal-oriented, intentional, data-driven comprehensive school counseling programs using evidence-based interventions (whenever possible). You also have the ability to grow, the ability to master these additional skills, and the ability to produce incredible results. Remember, this is about doing what is necessary to free you up to help additional students. We are producing and disseminating results to be able to do more school counseling! We share our results to earn freedom and time to implement additional school counseling interventions. We wish you the best in your own advocacy, in your own programming, and in your own pursuit of producing interventions that remove barriers to success for all students.

Appendix A

Belief Statement Examples

CAMPBELL COUNTY HIGH SCHOOL COUNSELING PROGRAM BELIEFS

- All students have significance and worth.
- All students—regardless of ability, age, gender, ethnicity, or sexual orientation—shall have equal access to all services (academic, career, and personal/social) provided by the counseling program and the school.
- All students learn best when positive relationships are present and fostered by all educational stakeholders.
- The school counseling program collaborates with educational stakeholders to increase equity and access to opportunity.
- The school counseling program serves a central role in meeting students' developmental needs through interventions in academic, career and personal/social domains.
- The school counseling program focuses on student learning and utilizes a data-driven comprehensive school counseling program to meet the needs of every student.
- The comprehensive school counseling program is tailored to meet students' developmental needs as identified through needs assessments, delivered using evidence-based programs, and evolved through data analysis of outcomes.

- The school counseling program utilizes the American School Counselor Association ethical standards.
- The comprehensive school counseling program is managed, delivered, and evaluated by certified professional school counselors to ensure maximum student achievement.
- School counselors must be leaders, advocates for every student, and collaborators who create equitable access to rigorous curriculum and opportunities for self-directed personal growth for every student.

CAMPBELL COUNTY MIDDLE SCHOOL COUNSELING PROGRAM BELIEFS

The school counselors at Campbell County Middle School believe:

- All students have significance and worth.
- All students—regardless of ability, age, gender, ethnicity, or sexual orientation—shall have equal access to all services (academic, career, and personal/social) provided by the counseling program and the school.
- All students have strengths that can be applied to achieve their goals.
- All students learn best when positive relationships are present and fostered by all educational stakeholders.
- School counselors must be advocates for every student.
- School counselors are leaders and change agents in school culture and academic achievement.
- School counselors develop positive relationships and recognize each student's special talents to help them achieve goals.
- The school counseling program collaborates with educational stakeholders to increase equity and access to opportunity.
- The school counseling program serves a central role in meeting students' developmental needs through interventions in academic, career, and personal/social domains.
- The school counseling program focuses on student learning and utilizes a data-driven comprehensive school counseling program to meet the needs of every student.
- The comprehensive school counseling program is tailored to meet students' developmental needs as identified through needs assessments,

delivered using evidence-based programs, and evolved through data analysis of outcomes.

- The school counseling program utilizes the American School Counselor Association ethical standards.

CLINE ELEMENTARY COUNSELING PROGRAM BELIEFS AND PHILOSOPHY

The counseling program at Cline Elementary believes:

- Education is a lifelong process in which individuals grow intellectually, socially, and emotionally.
- The school, home, and community are equally responsible for the educational development of our students.
- Each student is capable of working toward his/her unlimited potential in the following ways: intellectual, creative, artistic, social, physical, vocational, and emotional.
- Each student has the right and responsibility of equal access to all services (academic, career, and social/emotional) provided by the counseling department and the school, regardless of ethnic, cultural, racial, or sexual differences.

All counselors at Cline Elementary will:

- Abide by professional school counselor ethical standards and professional guidelines as specified by the ASCA National Model.
- Abide by ASCA suggestions of appropriate professional school counseling duties and coordinate with school administration to eliminate inappropriate school counseling duties currently implemented.
- Advocate for the academic, career, and personal/social well-being of all students.

DAYTON SCHOOL COUNSELING PROGRAM BELIEFS

The school counselors at Dayton High School believe:

- All students have significance and self-worth.

- All students—regardless of age, gender, race, ethnicity, or sexual orientation—shall have equal access to all services (academic, career, and personal/social) provided by the counseling program and the school.
- All students possess the ability to achieve with developmentally appropriate interventions.
- The school counseling program serves a central role in meeting students' developmental needs through interventions in academic, career, and personal/social domains.
- All students should have the opportunity to make choices within the constraints of the educational system.
- Student needs can be best met through an evidence-based, data-driven comprehensive school counseling program involving collaboration with all educational stakeholders, such as community members, parents, guardians, administration, teachers, and other student support personnel.
- Student achievement is maximized by participation in a comprehensive school counseling program that is planned, managed, delivered, and evaluated by certified professional school counselors.
- School counselors must be leaders, advocates for every student, and collaborators who create equitable access to rigorous curriculum and opportunities for self-directed personal growth for every student.
- The comprehensive school counseling program is tailored to meet students' developmental needs as identified through needs assessments, delivered using evidence-based programs when possible, and evolved through data analysis of outcomes.
- The American School Counselor Association ethical standards guide the work of the school counseling program and school counselors.

LINCOLN ELEMENTARY SCHOOL COUNSELING PROGRAM BELIEFS

- All students have significance and worth and deserve access to a positive learning environment.
- All students—regardless of ability, age, gender, ethnicity, or sexual orientation—shall have equal access to all services (academic, career, and personal/social) provided by the counseling program and the school.
- All students have strengths that can be applied to achieve their goals.

- All students learn best when positive relationships are present and fostered by all educational stakeholders.
- The school counselors adhere to the ethical standards provided by the American School Counselor Association.
- The school counselors provide valuable resources to be used in collaboration with educational stakeholders to increase equity and access to opportunity.
- The comprehensive school counseling program is tailored to meet students' developmental needs as identified through needs assessments, delivered using evidence-based programs, and evolved through data analysis of outcomes.
- The comprehensive school counseling program provides opportunities for students to form and express a personal vision, opportunities for students to develop positive relationships, and opportunities for students to recognize their own special talents to overcome barriers in their lives.

TICHENOR MIDDLE SCHOOL COUNSELING PROGRAM BELIEFS

The school counselors at Tichenor Middle School believe:

- School counselors must be advocates for every student.
- All students have significance and worth.
- All students—regardless of age, gender, race, ethnicity, or sexual orientation—shall have equal access to all services (academic, career, and personal/social) provided by the counseling program and the school.
- All students have strengths that can be applied to achieve their goals.
- The school counseling program serves a central role in meeting students' developmental needs through interventions in academic, career, and personal/social domains.
- Learning experiences should be created in such a way as to make them personally meaningful to students.
- Students need opportunities to form and express vision, develop positive mentorship relationships, and recognize their own special talents to overcome barriers in their lives.
- Student needs can be best met through a data-driven comprehensive school counseling program in collaboration with all educational stakeholders.

- The school counseling program provides valuable resources to be used in collaboration with educational stakeholders to increase equity and access to opportunity.
- School counselors are leaders and change agents in school culture and academic achievement.
- The comprehensive school counseling program is tailored to meet students' developmental needs as identified through needs assessments, delivered using evidence-based programs when possible, and evolved through data analysis of outcomes.
- The American School Counselor Association ethical standards guide the work of the school counseling program and school counselors.

Available for download at **http://www.corwin.com/ZyromskiEvidenceBased**

Appendix B

Mission Statement Examples

CAMPBELL COUNTY HIGH SCHOOL COUNSELING PROGRAM MISSION STATEMENT

The mission of the Campbell County High School Counseling Program is to lead all students to achieve college and/or career readiness standards. The comprehensive school counseling program collaborates with stakeholders to meet students' developmental needs as identified through needs assessments to deliver interventions using evidence-based program and evolves through data analysis and outcomes. Through the school counseling program, all students will be challenged to explore their passions, interests, and talents leading to increased engagement and continued growth. As a result, all students will be able to identify personal strengths that can be applied to achieve their academic, career, and personal/social goals.

CAMPBELL COUNTY MIDDLE SCHOOL COUNSELING PROGRAM MISSION STATEMENT

The mission of the Campbell County Middle School Counseling Program is to provide equal access for all students to a data-driven comprehensive school counseling program delivered by certified professional school counselors that meets the needs of every student. The comprehensive school counseling program collaborates with stakeholders to meet students' developmental needs as identified through needs assessments, to deliver interventions using evidence-based programs, and evolves through data analysis of outcomes.

As a result, all students will be able to identify personal strengths that can be applied to achieve their academic, career, and personal/social goals.

CLINE ELEMENTARY SCHOOL COUNSELING PROGRAM MISSION STATEMENT

The mission of the Cline Elementary School Counseling Program is to provide a data-driven comprehensive school counseling program that provides a safe, caring environment in which every student is engaged in successful lifelong learning. The comprehensive school counseling program collaborates with stakeholders such as teachers, administrators, Family Resource Coordinators, parents, caretakers, and other community members to meet students' developmental needs as identified through needs assessments and school report cards, to deliver interventions using evidence-based programs, and to evolve interventions through data analysis of outcomes. As a result, all students will identify individual strengths and developmental needs that they apply to achieve academic, college and career readiness, their personal/social goals, and to become lifelong learners.

LINCOLN ELEMENTARY SCHOOL COUNSELING PROGRAM MISSION STATEMENT

The mission of the Lincoln Elementary School Counseling Program is to increase equity and create opportunities for success for all students through empirically supported academic, career, and social/emotional programming, **INSPIRING** students to become life-long learners. The data-driven comprehensive school counseling program collaborates with other educational stakeholders, such as teachers, administrators, parents, families, caretakers, the family resource center, and other community stakeholders to **ENGAGE** all students in developmentally appropriate preventative and responsive counseling services resulting in academic, social/emotional, and college/career readiness **GROWTH**.

SHARP MIDDLE SCHOOL COUNSELING PROGRAM MISSION STATEMENT

The mission of the Sharp Middle School counseling program is to help prepare every student for success in the 21st century by removing barriers to achievement for all students through empirically supported academic, career, and social/personal programming. Through the school counseling program, all students are challenged to explore their passions, interests, and talents, leading to increased engagement and continued growth. The data-driven comprehensive school counseling program collaborates with other educational stakeholders, such as teachers, administrators, parents, families, caretakers, the family resources center, and other community stakeholders to provide developmentally appropriate preventative and responsive counseling services to all students resulting in increases in achievement academically, personally, and in post-secondary college and career pursuits.

TICHENOR MIDDLE SCHOOL COUNSELING PROGRAM MISSION STATEMENT

Welcome to the Tichenor Middle School Counseling Department webpage!

For updates about what we are doing at Tichenor Middle School, please visit:

http://www.TMSCounselors.blogspot.com

Tichenor Middle School has two full-time school counselors:

Angie Bielecki, MEd: Students A–K

Mrs. Bielecki has been a school counselor with the Erlanger-Elsmere school district since 2007. She received a Bachelor of Arts degree from Colorado College in Sociology and a Master of Education degree from the University of Cincinnati in School Counseling. She began her work as a school counselor in Cincinnati and is passionate about helping schools, families, and students come together. She enjoys running, music, reading, and being outside. If Mrs. Bielecki had one super power, she would choose being able to teleport herself so she never has to sit in traffic.

Amy Gillio, MA: Students L–Z

Ms. Gillio has been a school counselor with the Erlanger-Elsmere school district since 2012. She received a Bachelor of Science degree from the University of Pittsburgh in Psychology and her Master of Arts degree from Xavier University in School Counseling. Through a variety of community service projects and internship experiences, Ms. Gillio developed a passion for working with children and their communities. She enjoys tennis, cooking, and local sporting events. If Ms. Gillio was ever stuck on a deserted island, she would like to have with her chapstick, an iPhone, and a good book!

Vision Statement

We promote the importance of safety, respect, and responsibility for all individuals at Tichenor Middle School.

Mission Statement

Within a safe, respectful, and responsible environment, TMS School counselors provide a developmental program to encourage and support the academic, social, and emotional growth for all students and their plans for the future.

Current Tichenor School Counseling Program Components

Advisory: Every student at Tichenor Middle School will participate in a 25-minute daily advisory class. This year we are piloting this program as time to develop skills in academic, social, and career planning areas. Classes are gender-based, under twenty students, and led by classroom teachers.

Small Group and Individual Counseling: Trained school counselors can deliver individual student services and small group services to students who request it or have been referred.

Support Services: School counselors collaborate with outside agencies, community resources, and district staff to help connect students and promote success.

Available for download at **http://www.corwin.com/ZyromskiEvidenceBased**

Appendix C

Needs Assessments

GRADES 6–8 TOTAL NEEDS RESULTS

Grades 6–8 Total							
		#	%			#	%
1	Coping with stress	27	**13.6**	21	Fear of making mistakes	34	**17.2**
2	Difficulty controlling anger	52	**26.3**	22	Skipping school	24	**12.1**
3	Receiving one or more failing grades on a report card	36	**18.2**	23	Test anxiety and test-taking skills	27	**13.6**
4	Fights	97	**49.0**	24	Not getting along with teachers	48	**24.2**
5	Student use of alcohol or drugs	38	**19.2**	25	Domestic violence	11	**5.6**
6	A divorce or family separation	23	**11.6**	26	Impairment or disability	2	**1.0**
7	Bullying or harassment	92	**46.5**	27	Communication problems	7	**3.5**
8	Loss of a close friend or relationship	33	**16.7**	28	Physical or sexual abuse	7	**3.5**
9	Exploring career options	12	**6.1**	29	Neglect	9	**4.5**
10	Different values between generations	2	**1.0**	30	Attention in class or on school work	33	**16.7**
11	Dealing with people of a different ethnicity, race, or religion	10	**5.1**	31	Homelessness	2	**1.0**
12	Drug or alcohol abuse in the family	13	**6.6**	32	Rumors and gossip	89	**44.9**
13	Learning about college opportunities	18	**9.1**	33	Major health concerns in family	4	**2.0**
14	Thinking or talking about suicide	20	**10.1**	34	Low self-regard	2	**1.0**
15	Feeling sad or depressed a lot	34	**17.2**	35	Trouble getting along with friends or others	16	**8.1**
16	Poverty	11	**5.6**	36	Death of a loved one	19	**9.6**
17	Dropping out of school	8	**4.0**	37	Hurting or cutting oneself	35	**17.7**
18	Problems with eating or body image	18	**9.1**	38	Adjusting to a new place or culture	7	**3.5**
19	Gender or sexual orientation issues	3	**1.5**	39	Setting and carrying out goals	18	**9.1**
20	Time management and organization	25	**12.6**	40	Teenage pregnancy	22	**11.1**

1 **Fights** *(49.0% of those polled list this as a concern)*

2 **Bullying or harassment** *(46.5% of those polled list this as a concern)*

3 **Rumors and gossip** *(44.9% of those polled list this as a concern)*

4 **Difficulty controlling anger** *(26.3% of those polled list this as a concern)*

5 **Not getting along with teachers** *(24.2% of those polled list this as a concern)*

Most Common Student Frustrations: Gossip — Bullying — Maintaining Friendships — Grades/Homework — Future plans

Counselor Can Help by: Stopping bullying — Talking to students about their problems — Encouragement — Helping with organization/time management — "I don't know"

GRADE 6 NEEDS RESULTS

Grade 6 Total							
		#	%			#	%
1	Coping with stress	6	**8.7**	21	Fear of making mistakes	14	**20.3**
2	Difficulty controlling anger	21	**30.4**	22	Skipping school	10	**14.5**
3	Receiving one or more failing grades on a report card	18	**26.1**	23	Test anxiety and test-taking skills	13	**18.8**
4	Fights	33	47.8	24	Not getting along with teachers	16	**23.2**
5	Student use of alcohol or drugs	11	**15.9**	25	Domestic violence	6	**8.7**
6	A divorce or family separation	10	**14.5**	26	Impairment or disability	0	**0.0**
7	Bullying or harassment	20	**29.0**	27	Communication problems	2	**2.9**
8	Loss of a close friend or relationship	10	**14.5**	28	Physical or sexual abuse	2	**2.9**
9	Exploring career options	3	**4.3**	29	Neglect	4	**5.8**
10	Different values between generations	0	**0.0**	30	Attention in class or on school work	11	**15.9**
11	Dealing with people of a different ethnicity, race, or religion	2	**2.9**	31	Homelessness	1	**1.4**
12	Drug or alcohol abuse in the family	2	**2.9**	32	Rumors and gossip	25	**36.2**
13	Learning about college opportunities	7	**10.1**	33	Major health concerns in family	1	**1.4**
14	Thinking or talking about suicide	12	**17.4**	34	Low self-regard	1	**1.4**
15	Feeling sad or depressed a lot	9	**13.0**	35	Trouble getting along with friends or others	6	**8.7**
16	Poverty	2	**2.9**	36	Death of a loved one	8	**11.6**
17	Dropping out of school	2	**2.9**	37	Hurting or cutting oneself	16	**23.2**
18	Problems with eating or body image	6	**8.7**	38	Adjusting to a new place or culture	3	**4.3**
19	Gender or sexual orientation issues	2	**2.9**	39	Setting and carrying out goals	7	**10.1**
20	Time management and organization	12	**17.4**	40	Teenage pregnancy	10	**14.5**

1 **Fights** *(47.8% of those polled list this as a concern)*

2 **Rumors and gossip** *(36.2% of those polled list this as a concern)*

3 **Difficulty controlling anger** *(30.4% of those polled list this as a concern)*

4 **Bullying or harassment** *(29.0% of those polled list this as a concern)*

5 **Receiving one or more failing grades** *(26.1% of those polled list this as a concern)*

Most Common Student Frustrations: Gossip — Bullying — Transition from elementary — Friends *(making them and keeping them)*

Counselor Can Help by: Stoping bullying — Talking to students about their problems — Helping with organization/time management — "I don't know"

Grade 6 Boys							
		#	%			#	%
1	Coping with stress	2	**6.9**	21	Fear of making mistakes	4	**13.8**
2	Difficulty controlling anger	9	**31.0**	22	Skipping school	4	**13.8**
3	Receiving one or more failing grades on a report card	7	**24.1**	23	Test anxiety and test-taking skills	5	**17.2**
4	Fights	19	**65.5**	24	Not getting along with teachers	7	**24.1**
5	Student use of alcohol or drugs	6	**20.7**	25	Domestic violence	2	**6.9**
6	A divorce or family separation	8	**27.6**	26	Impairment or disability	0	**0.0**
7	Bullying or harassment	8	**27.6**	27	Communication problems	1	**3.4**
8	Loss of a close friend or relationship	1	**3.4**	28	Physical or sexual abuse	1	**3.4**
9	Exploring career options	3	**10.3**	29	Neglect	2	**6.9**
10	Different values between generations	0	**0.0**	30	Attention in class or on school work	4	**13.8**
11	Dealing with people of a different ethnicity, race, or religion	0	**0.0**	31	Homelessness	0	**0.0**
12	Drug or alcohol abuse in the family	1	**3.4**	32	Rumors and gossip	6	**20.7**
13	Learning about college opportunities	5	**17.2**	33	Major health concerns in family	1	**3.4**
14	Thinking or talking about suicide	4	**13.8**	34	Low self-regard	1	**3.4**
15	Feeling sad or depressed a lot	1	**3.4**	35	Trouble getting along with friends or others	3	**10.3**
16	Poverty	0	**0.0**	36	Death of a loved one	6	**20.7**
17	Dropping out of school	1	**3.4**	37	Hurting or cutting oneself	7	**24.1**
18	Problems with eating or body image	2	**6.9**	38	Adjusting to a new place or culture	1	**3.4**
19	Gender or sexual orientation issues	3	**10.3**	39	Setting and carrying out goals	2	**6.9**
20	Time management and organization	3	**10.3**	40	Teenage pregnancy	3	**10.3**

1	**Fights** *(65.5% of those polled list this as a concern)*
2	**Difficulty controlling anger** *(31.0% of those polled list this as a concern)*
3	**Bullying or harassment** *(27.6% of those polled list this as a concern)*
4	**Divorce or family separation** *(27% of those polled list this as a concern)*
5	**Failing/self-harm/teacher conflict** *(24.1% list this as a concern)*

Grade 6 Girls							
		#	%			#	%
1	Coping with stress	4	**9.8**	21	Fear of making mistakes	10	**24.4**
2	Difficulty controlling anger	12	**29.3**	22	Skipping school	6	**14.6**
3	Receiving one or more failing grades on a report card	11	**26.8**	23	Test anxiety and test-taking skills	8	**19.5**
4	Fights	14	34.1	24	Not getting along with teachers	9	**22.0**
5	Student use of alcohol or drugs	5	**12.2**	25	Domestic violence	4	**9.8**
6	A divorce or family separation	2	**4.9**	26	Impairment or disability	0	**0.0**
7	Bullying or harassment	12	**29.3**	27	Communication problems	1	**2.4**
8	Loss of a close friend or relationship	9	**22.0**	28	Physical or sexual abuse	1	**2.4**
9	Exploring career options	0	**0.0**	29	Neglect	2	**4.9**
10	Different values between generations	0	**0.0**	30	Attention in class or on school work	7	**17.1**
11	Dealing with people of a different ethnicity, race, or religion	2	**4.9**	31	Homelessness	1	**2.4**
12	Drug or alcohol abuse in the family	1	**2.4**	32	Rumors and gossip	19	**46.3**
13	Learning about college opportunities	2	**4.9**	33	Major health concerns in family	0	**0.0**
14	Thinking or talking about suicide	8	**19.5**	34	Low self-regard	0	**0.0**
15	Feeling sad or depressed a lot	8	**19.5**	35	Trouble getting along with friends or others	3	**7.3**
16	Poverty	2	**4.9**	36	Death of a loved one	2	**4.9**
17	Dropping out of school	1	**2.4**	37	Hurting or cutting oneself	9	**22.0**
18	Problems with eating or body image	4	**9.8**	38	Adjusting to a new place or culture	2	**4.9**
19	Gender or sexual orientation issues	1	**2.4**	39	Setting and carrying out goals	5	**12.2**
20	Time management and organization	9	**22.0**	40	Teenage pregnancy	7	**17.1**
1	**Rumors and gossip** *(36.2% of those polled list this as a concern)*						
2	**Fights** *(65.5% of those polled list this as a concern)*						
3	**Difficulty controlling anger** *(31.0% of those polled list this as a concern)*						
4	**Bullying or harassment** *(27.6% of those polled list this as a concern)*						
5	**Receiving one or more failing grades** *(26.1% of those polled list this as a concern)*						

GRADE 7 NEEDS RESULTS

Grade 7 Total							
		#	%			#	%
1	Coping with stress	6	**9.1**	21	Fear of making mistakes	10	**15.2**
2	Difficulty controlling anger	17	**25.8**	22	Skipping school	7	**10.6**
3	Receiving one or more failing grades on a report card	12	**18.2**	23	Test anxiety and test-taking skills	4	**6.1**
4	Fights	44	**66.7**	24	Not getting along with teachers	17	**25.8**
5	Student use of alcohol or drugs	14	**21.2**	25	Domestic violence	2	**3.0**
6	A divorce or family separation	6	**9.1**	26	Impairment or disability	1	**1.5**
7	Bullying or harassment	42	**63.6**	27	Communication problems	1	**1.5**
8	Loss of a close friend or relationship	12	**18.2**	28	Physical or sexual abuse	4	**6.1**
9	Exploring career options	2	**3.0**	29	Neglect	3	**4.5**
10	Different values between generations	1	**1.5**	30	Attention in class or on school work	13	**19.7**
11	Dealing with people of a different ethnicity, race, or religion	3	**4.5**	31	Homelessness	1	**1.5**
12	Drug or alcohol abuse in the family	5	**7.6**	32	Rumors and gossip	31	**47.0**
13	Learning about college opportunities	3	**4.5**	33	Major health concerns in family	2	**3.0**
14	Thinking or talking about suicide	5	**7.6**	34	Low self-regard	1	**1.5**
15	Feeling sad or depressed a lot	9	**13.6**	35	Trouble getting along with friends or others	6	**9.1**
16	Poverty	3	**4.5**	36	Death of a loved one	9	**13.6**
17	Dropping out of school	6	**9.1**	37	Hurting or cutting oneself	1	**1.5**
18	Problems with eating or body image	5	**7.6**	38	Adjusting to a new place or culture	3	**4.5**
19	Gender or sexual orientation issues	0	**0.0**	39	Setting and carrying out goals	4	**6.1**
20	Time management and organization	5	**7.6**	40	Teenage pregnancy	10	**15.2**

1 **Fights** *(66.7% of those polled list this as a concern)*

2 **Bullying or harassment** *(63.6% of those polled list this as a concern)*

3 **Rumors and gossip** *(47.0% of those polled list this as a concern)*

4 **Difficulty controlling anger** *(25.8% of those polled list this as a concern)*

5 **Not getting along with teachers** *(25.8% list this as a concern)*

Most Common Student Frustrations: Bullying — Homework

Counselor Can Help by: Talking to students about their problems — Encouragement — Anger management — "I don't know"

Grade 7 Boys							
		#	%			#	%
1	Coping with stress	3	**6.9**	21	Fear of making mistakes	7	**16.1**
2	Difficulty controlling anger	14	**32.1**	22	Skipping school	7	**16.1**
3	Receiving one or more failing grades on a report card	5	**11.5**	23	Test anxiety and test-taking skills	0	**0.0**
4	Fights	30	**68.8**	24	Not getting along with teachers	10	**22.9**
5	Student use of alcohol or drugs	9	**20.6**	25	Domestic violence	1	**2.3**
6	A divorce or family separation	3	**6.9**	26	Impairment or disability	1	**2.3**
7	Bullying or harassment	29	**66.5**	27	Communication problems	1	**2.3**
8	Loss of a close friend or relationship	7	**16.1**	28	Physical or sexual abuse	3	**6.9**
9	Exploring career options	1	**2.3**	29	Neglect	3	**6.9**
10	Different values between generations	1	**2.3**	30	Attention in class or on school work	10	**22.9**
11	Dealing with people of a different ethnicity, race, or religion	3	**6.9**	31	Homelessness	1	**2.3**
12	Drug or alcohol abuse in the family	4	**9.2**	32	Rumors and gossip	15	**34.4**
13	Learning about college opportunities	2	**4.6**	33	Major health concerns in family	2	**4.6**
14	Thinking or talking about suicide	3	**6.9**	34	Low self-regard	1	**2.3**
15	Feeling sad or depressed a lot	7	**16.1**	35	Trouble getting along with friends or others	2	**4.6**
16	Poverty	2	**4.6**	36	Death of a loved one	7	**16.1**
17	Dropping out of school	3	**6.9**	37	Hurting or cutting oneself	0	**0.0**
18	Problems with eating or body image	5	**11.5**	38	Adjusting to a new place or culture	3	**6.9**
19	Gender or sexual orientation issues	0	**0.0**	39	Setting and carrying out goals	2	**4.6**
20	Time management and organization	5	**11.5**	40	Teenage pregnancy	6	**13.8**

1 **Fights** *(68.8% of those polled list this as a concern)*
2 **Bullying or harassment** *(66.5% of those polled list this as a concern)*
3 **Rumors and gossip** *(34.4% of those polled list this as a concern)*
4 **Difficulty controlling anger** *(32.1% of those polled list this as a concern)*
5 **Attention in class/teacher conflict** *(22.9% list this as a concern)*

Grade 7 Girls							
		#	%			#	%
1	Coping with stress	3	**11.3**	21	Fear of making mistakes	3	**11.3**
2	Difficulty controlling anger	3	**11.3**	22	Skipping school	0	**0.0**
3	Receiving one or more failing grades on a report card	7	**26.3**	23	Test anxiety and test-taking skills	4	**15.0**
4	Fights	14	**52.6**	24	Not getting along with teachers	7	**26.3**
5	Student use of alcohol or drugs	5	**18.8**	25	Domestic violence	1	**3.8**
6	A divorce or family separation	3	**11.3**	26	Impairment or disability	0	**0.0**
7	Bullying or harassment	13	**48.9**	27	Communication problems	0	**0.0**
8	Loss of a close friend or relationship	5	**18.8**	28	Physical or sexual abuse	1	**3.8**
9	Exploring career options	1	**3.8**	29	Neglect	0	**0.0**
10	Different values between generations	0	**0.0**	30	Attention in class or on school work	3	**11.3**
11	Dealing with people of a different ethnicity, race, or religion	0	**0.0**	31	Homelessness	0	**0.0**
12	Drug or alcohol abuse in the family	1	**3.8**	32	Rumors and gossip	16	**60.2**
13	Learning about college opportunities	1	**3.8**	33	Major health concerns in family	0	**0.0**
14	Thinking or talking about suicide	2	**7.5**	34	Low self-regard	0	**0.0**
15	Feeling sad or depressed a lot	2	**7.5**	35	Trouble getting along with friends or others	4	**15.0**
16	Poverty	1	**3.8**	36	Death of a loved one	2	**7.5**
17	Dropping out of school	3	**11.3**	37	Hurting or cutting oneself	1	**3.8**
18	Problems with eating or body image	0	**0.0**	38	Adjusting to a new place or culture	0	**0.0**
19	Gender or sexual orientation issues	0	**0.0**	39	Setting and carrying out goals	2	**7.5**
20	Time management and organization	1	**3.8**	40	Teenage pregnancy	4	**15.0**

1 **Rumors and gossip** *(60.2% of those polled list this as a concern)*

2 **Fights** *(52.6% of those polled list this as a concern)*

3 **Bullying or harassment** *(48.9% of those polled list this as a concern)*

4 **Receiving failing grades** *(26.3% of those polled list this as a concern)*

5 **Not getting along with teachers** *(26.3% list this as a concern)*

GRADE 8 NEEDS RESULTS

Grade 8 Total							
		#	%			#	%
1	Coping with stress	15	**23.9**	21	Fear of making mistakes	10	**15.9**
2	Difficulty controlling anger	14	**22.3**	22	Skipping school	7	**11.1**
3	Receiving one or more failing grades on a report card	6	**9.6**	23	Test anxiety and test-taking skills	10	**15.9**
4	Fights	20	**31.8**	24	Not getting along with teachers	15	**23.9**
5	Student use of alcohol or drugs	13	**20.7**	25	Domestic violence	3	**4.8**
6	A divorce or family separation	7	**11.1**	26	Impairment or disability	1	**1.6**
7	Bullying or harassment	30	**47.8**	27	Communication problems	4	**6.4**
8	Loss of a close friend or relationship	11	**17.5**	28	Physical or sexual abuse	1	**1.6**
9	Exploring career options	7	**11.1**	29	Neglect	2	**3.2**
10	Different values between generations	1	**1.6**	30	Attention in class or on school work	9	**14.3**
11	Dealing with people of a different ethnicity, race, or religion	5	**8.0**	31	Homelessness	0	**0.0**
12	Drug or alcohol abuse in the family	6	**9.6**	32	Rumors and gossip	33	**52.5**
13	Learning about college opportunities	8	**12.7**	33	Major health concerns in family	1	**1.6**
14	Thinking or talking about suicide	3	**4.8**	34	Low self-regard	0	**0.0**
15	Feeling sad or depressed a lot	16	**25.5**	35	Trouble getting along with friends or others	4	**6.4**
16	Poverty	6	**9.6**	36	Death of a loved one	2	**3.2**
17	Dropping out of school	0	**0.0**	37	Hurting or cutting oneself	18	**28.7**
18	Problems with eating or body image	7	**11.1**	38	Adjusting to a new place or culture	1	**1.6**
19	Gender or sexual orientation issues	1	**1.6**	39	Setting and carrying out goals	7	**11.1**
20	Time management and organization	8	**12.7**	40	Teenage pregnancy	2	**3.2**

1 **Rumors and gossip** *(52.5% of those polled list this as a concern)*

2 **Bullying or harassment** *(47.8% of those polled list this as a concern)*

3 **Fights** *(31.8% of those polled list this as a concern)*

4 **Hurting or cutting oneself** *(28.7% of those polled list this as a concern)*

5 **Feeling sad or depressed a lot** *(25.5% of those polled list this as a concern)*

Most Common Student Frustrations: Bullying — Gossip — Grades — My future plans

Counselor Can Help by: Someone to talk to — Encouragement — Anger management — Coping with stress — Planning my future

Grade 8 Boys							
		#	%			#	%
1	Coping with stress	6	**16.2**	21	Fear of making mistakes	6	**16.2**
2	Difficulty controlling anger	10	**27.0**	22	Skipping school	5	**13.5**
3	Receiving one or more failing grades on a report card	4	**10.8**	23	Test anxiety and test-taking skills	8	**21.6**
4	Fights	11	**29.7**	24	Not getting along with teachers	10	**27.0**
5	Student use of alcohol or drugs	8	**21.6**	25	Domestic violence	2	**5.4**
6	A divorce or family separation	7	**18.9**	26	Impairment or disability	0	**0.0**
7	Bullying or harassment	14	**37.8**	27	Communication problems	3	**8.1**
8	Loss of a close friend or relationship	5	**13.5**	28	Physical or sexual abuse	1	**2.7**
9	Exploring career options	4	**10.8**	29	Neglect	2	**5.4**
10	Different values between generations	0	**0.0**	30	Attention in class or on school work	6	**16.2**
11	Dealing with people of a different ethnicity, race, or religion	5	**13.5**	31	Homelessness	0	**0.0**
12	Drug or alcohol abuse in the family	6	**16.2**	32	Rumors and gossip	20	**54.1**
13	Learning about college opportunities	3	**8.1**	33	Major health concerns in family	1	**2.7**
14	Thinking or talking about suicide	1	**2.7**	34	Low self-regard	0	**0.0**
15	Feeling sad or depressed a lot	5	**13.5**	35	Trouble getting along with friends or others	2	**5.4**
16	Poverty	5	**13.5**	36	Death of a loved one	2	**5.4**
17	Dropping out of school	0	**0.0**	37	Hurting or cutting oneself	7	**18.9**
18	Problems with eating or body image	1	**2.7**	38	Adjusting to a new place or culture	1	**2.7**
19	Gender or sexual orientation issues	1	**2.7**	39	Setting and carrying out goals	6	**16.2**
20	Time management and organization	6	**16.2**	40	Teenage pregnancy	1	**2.7**

1 **Rumors and gossip** *(54.1% of those polled list this as a concern)*
2 **Bullying or harassment** *(37.8% of those polled list this as a concern)*
3 **Fights** *(29.7% of those polled list this as a concern)*
4 **Difficulty controlling anger** *(27.0% of those polled list this as a concern)*
5 **Not getting along with teachers** *(27.0% of those polled list this as a concern)*

Grade 8 Girls							
		#	%			#	%
1	Coping with stress	9	**34.9**	21	Fear of making mistakes	4	**15.5**
2	Difficulty controlling anger	4	**15.5**	22	Skipping school	2	**7.8**
3	Receiving one or more failing grades on a report card	2	**7.8**	23	Test anxiety and test-taking skills	2	**7.8**
4	Fights	9	**34.9**	24	Not getting along with teachers	5	**19.4**
5	Student use of alcohol or drugs	5	**19.4**	25	Domestic violence	1	**3.9**
6	A divorce or family separation	0	**0.0**	26	Impairment or disability	1	**3.9**
7	Bullying or harassment	16	**62.0**	27	Communication problems	1	**3.9**
8	Loss of a close friend or relationship	6	**23.3**	28	Physical or sexual abuse	0	**0.0**
9	Exploring career options	3	**11.6**	29	Neglect	0	**0.0**
10	Different values between generations	1	**3.9**	30	Attention in class or on school work	3	**11.6**
11	Dealing with people of a different ethnicity, race, or religion	0	**0.0**	31	Homelessness	0	**0.0**
12	Drug or alcohol abuse in the family	0	**0.0**	32	Rumors and gossip	13	**50.4**
13	Learning about college opportunities	5	**19.4**	33	Major health concerns in family	0	**0.0**
14	Thinking or talking about suicide	2	**7.8**	34	Low self-regard	0	**0.0**
15	Feeling sad or depressed a lot	11	**42.6**	35	Trouble getting along with friends or others	2	**7.8**
16	Poverty	1	**3.9**	36	Death of a loved one	0	**0.0**
17	Dropping out of school	0	**0.0**	37	Hurting or cutting oneself	11	**42.6**
18	Problems with eating or body image	6	**23.3**	38	Adjusting to a new place or culture	0	**0.0**
19	Gender or sexual orientation issues	0	**0.0**	39	Setting and carrying out goals	1	**3.9**
20	Time management and organization	2	**7.8**	40	Teenage pregnancy	1	**3.9**
1	**Bullying or harassment** *(62.0% of those polled list this as a concern)*						
2	**Rumors and gossip** *(50.4% of those polled list this as a concern)*						
3	**Hurting or cutting oneself** *(42.6% of those polled list this as a concern)*						
4	**Feeling sad or depressed a lot** *(42.6% of those polled list this as a concern)*						
5	**Fights/coping with stress** *(34.9% of those polled list this as a concern)*						

TEACHER NEEDS RESULTS

Faculty/Staff Total							
		#	%				
1	Coping with stress	2	**11.6**	21	Fear of making mistakes	0	**0.0**
2	Difficulty controlling anger	7	**40.7**	22	Skipping school	0	**0.0**
3	Receiving one or more failing grades on a report card	0	**0.0**	23	Test anxiety and test-taking skills	2	**11.6**
4	Fights	6	**34.9**	24	Not getting along with teachers	1	**5.8**
5	Student use of alcohol or drugs	0	**0.0**	25	Domestic violence	0	**0.0**
6	A divorce or family separation	2	**11.6**	26	Impairment or disability	0	**0.0**
7	Bullying or harassment	2	**11.6**	27	Communication problems	1	**5.8**
8	Loss of a close friend or relationship	0	**0.0**	28	Physical or sexual abuse	0	**0.0**
9	Exploring career options	0	**0.0**	29	Neglect	9	**52.3**
10	Different values between generations	1	**5.8**	30	Attention in class or on school work	13	**75.6**
11	Dealing with people of a different ethnicity, race, or religion	0	**0.0**	31	Homelessness	0	**0.0**
12	Drug or alcohol abuse in the family	5	**29.1**	32	Rumors and gossip	2	**11.6**
13	Learning about college opportunities	0	**0.0**	33	Major health concerns in family	0	**0.0**
14	Thinking or talking about suicide	0	**0.0**	34	Low self-regard	3	**17.4**
15	Feeling sad or depressed a lot	1	**5.8**	35	Trouble getting along with friends or others	5	**29.1**
16	Poverty	8	**46.5**	36	Death of a loved one	0	**0.0**
17	Dropping out of school	1	**5.8**	37	Hurting or cutting oneself	0	**0.0**
18	Problems with eating or body image	0	**0.0**	38	Adjusting to a new place or culture	0	**0.0**
19	Gender or sexual orientation issues	0	**0.0**	39	Setting and carrying out goals	3	**17.4**
20	Time management and organization	12	**69.8**	40	Teenage pregnancy	0	**0.0**

1 **Attention in class or on school work** *(75.6% of those polled list this as a concern)*
2 **Time management and organization** *(69.8% of those polled list this as a concern)*
3 **Neglect** *(52.3% of those polled list this as a concern)*
4 **Poverty** *(46.5% of those polled list this as a concern)*
5 **Difficulty controlling anger** *(40.7% of those polled list this as a concern)*

Most Common Frustrations: Lack of student motivation/focus — Student defiance/attitude — Class sizes

Counselor Can Help by: Student motivation — Anger/stress coping skills — Social skills — Time management/organization — Increasing parent involvement

Greatest Strength: Faculty and staff that care, put students first, work together, and listen

STUDENT NEEDS ASSESSMENT

DO NOT PUT YOUR NAME

Middle School Student Needs Assessment

What is your greatest strength? ______________________________________

____

Grade ________________ Male or Female (circle one)

Based on your experience and knowledge, please check the concerns that *slow* the learning and growth of SMS students. Please check the top five issues that worry you the most. Then circle the greatest one concern of those five.

	Concerns	Check		Concerns	Check
1	Coping with stress		11	Dealing with people of a different ethnicity, race, or religion	
2	Difficulty controlling anger		12	Drug or alcohol abuse in the family	
3	Receiving one or more failing grades on a report card		13	Learning about college opportunities	
4	Fights		14	Thinking or talking about suicide	
5	Student use of alcohol or drugs		15	Feeling sad or depressed a lot	
6	A divorce or family separation		16	Poverty	
7	Bullying or harassment		17	Dropping out of school	
8	Loss of a close friend or relationship		18	Problems with eating or body image	
9	Exploring career options		19	Gender or sexual orientation issues	
10	Different values between generations		20	Time management and organization	

	Concerns	Check		Concerns	Check
21	Fear of making mistakes		31	Homelessness	
22	Skipping school		32	Rumors and gossip	
23	Test anxiety and test-taking skills		33	Major health concerns in family	
24	Not getting along with teachers		34	Low self-regard	
25	Domestic violence		35	Trouble getting along with friends or others	
26	Impairment or disability		36	Death of a loved one	
27	Communication problems		37	Hurting or cutting oneself	
28	Physical or sexual abuse		38	Adjusting to a new place or culture	
29	Neglect		39	Setting and carrying out goals	
30	Attention in class or on school work		40	Teenage pregnancy	

Are there any others? Please list them.

____

____

What is your biggest frustration as a student at SMS?

____

____

How can your school counselor help you to be more successful?

____

____

TEACHER NEEDS ASSESSMENT

DO NOT PUT YOUR NAME

Middle School Teacher Needs Assessment

What is the greatest strength of SMS? ________________________________

____

Based on your experience and knowledge, please check the concerns that *slow* the learning and growth of SMS students. Please check the top five issues that worry you the most. Then circle the greatest one concern of those five.

	Concerns	Check		Concerns	Check
1	Coping with stress		11	Dealing with people of a different ethnicity, race, or religion	
2	Difficulty controlling anger		12	Drug or alcohol abuse in the family	
3	Receiving one or more failing grades on a report card		13	Learning about college opportunities	
4	Fights		14	Thinking or talking about suicide	
5	Student use of alcohol or drugs		15	Feeling sad or depressed a lot	
6	A divorce or family separation		16	Poverty	
7	Bullying or harassment		17	Dropping out of school	
8	Loss of a close friend or relationship		18	Problems with eating or body image	
9	Exploring career options		19	Gender or sexual orientation issues	
10	Different values between generations		20	Time management and organization	

	Concerns	Check		Concerns	Check
21	Fear of making mistakes		31	Homelessness	
22	Skipping school		32	Rumors and gossip	
23	Test anxiety and test-taking skills		33	Major health concerns in family	
24	Not getting along with teachers		34	Low self-regard	
25	Domestic violence		35	Trouble getting along with friends or others	
26	Impairment or disability		36	Death of a loved one	
27	Communication problems		37	Hurting or cutting oneself	
28	Physical or sexual abuse		38	Adjusting to a new place or culture	
29	Neglect		39	Setting and carrying out goals	
30	Attention in class or on school work		40	Teenage pregnancy	

Are there any others? Please list them.

____

____

What is your biggest frustration as a teacher at SMS?

____

____

What can the school counseling department do (or do better) to ensure student success?

____

____

Please return to the envelope marked "Completed Needs Assessments" near your mailbox.

STUDENT–FACULTY DIFFERENCE NEEDS RESULTS

Difference (Student–Faculty)		Difference (Student–Faculty)	
Coping with stress	7.54	Fear of making mistakes	17.17
Difficulty controlling anger	–10.32	Skipping school	12.12
Receiving one or more failing grades on a report card	18.18	Test anxiety and test-taking skills	1.44
Fights	12.40	Not getting along with teachers	18.14
Student use of alcohol or drugs	19.19	Domestic violence	5.56
A divorce or family separation	–0.58	Impairment or disability	1.01
Bullying or harassment	34.27	Communication problems	–2.56
Loss of a close friend or relationship	16.67	Physical or sexual abuse	3.54
Exploring career options	6.06	Neglect	–50.33
Different values between generations	–5.09	Attention in class or on school work	–62.60
Dealing with people of a different ethnicity, race, or religion	5.05	Homelessness	1.01
Drug or alcohol abuse in the family	–23.92	Rumors and gossip	38.85
Learning about college opportunities	9.09	Major health concerns in family	2.02
Thinking or talking about suicide	10.10	Low self-regard	–17.28
Feeling sad or depressed a lot	11.07	Trouble getting along with friends or others	–22.41
Poverty	–37.13	Death of a loved one	9.60
Dropping out of school	–2.06	Hurting or cutting oneself	17.68
Problems with eating or body image	9.09	Adjusting to a new place or culture	3.54
Gender or sexual orientation issues	1.52	Setting and carrying out goals	–9.20
Time management and organization	–60.54	Teenage pregnancy	11.11

Available for download at **http://www.corwin.com/ZyromskiEvidenceBased**

References

American School Counselor Association. (2012). *The ASCA national model: A framework for school counseling programs* (3rd ed.). Alexandria, VA: Author.

American School Counselor Association. (2014). Recognized ASCA Model Program (RAMP) scoring rubric. Alexandria, VA: Author. Retrieved from http://www.ascanationalmodel.org/learn-about- ramp/ramp-rubric

Austin, S., & Joseph, S. (1996). Assessment of bully/victim problems in 8–11 year-olds. *British Journal of Educational Psychology, 66*, 447–456.

Bronson, M. B., Goodson, B. D., Layzer, J. I., & Love, J. M. (1990). *Child behavior rating scale*. Cambridge, MA: Abt Associates.

Carey, J., Brigman, G., Webb, L., Villares, E., & Harrington, K. (2013). Development of an instrument to measure student use of academic success skills: An exploratory factor analysis [advance online publication]. *Measurement and Evaluation in Counseling and Development*. doi:10.1177/0748175613505622

Carey, J., & Dimmitt, C. (2012). School counseling and student outcomes: Summary of six statewide studies. *Professional School Counseling, 16*(2), 146–153.

Carey, J., Harrington, K., Martin, I., & Hoffman, D. (2012). A statewide evaluation of the outcomes of ASCA National Model school counseling programs in rural and suburban Nebraska high schools. *Professional School Counseling, 16*, 100–107.

Carey, J., Harrington, K., Martin, I., & Stevenson, D. (2012). A statewide evaluation of the outcomes of the implementation of ASCA National Model school counseling programs in Utah high schools. *Professional School Counseling, 16*, 89–99.

Carrell, S. E., & Hoekstra, M. (2011). Are school counselors a cost-effective education input? Retrieved from http://dx.doi.org/10.2139/ssrn.1629868

Crick, N. R., & Grotpeter, J. K. (1995). Relational aggression, gender, and social-psychological adjustment. *Child Development, 66*(3), 710–722.

Dahir, C. A., & Stone, C. B. (2012). *The transformed school counselor*. Boston, MA: Cengage.

Dimmitt, C., Carey, J. C., & Hatch, T. (2007). *Evidence-based school counseling: Making a difference with data-driven practices*. Thousand Oaks, CA: Corwin.

Dimmitt, C., Wilkerson, B., & Lapan, R. (2012). Comprehensive school counseling in Rhode Island: Access to services and student outcomes. *Professional School Counseling, 16*, 125–135.

Elliott, S. N., & Gresham, F. M. (2007). *SSIS performance screening guide.* Minneapolis, MN: NCS Pearson.

Finn, J. D., Folger, J., & Cox, D. (1991). Measuring participation among elementary grade students. *Educational & Psychological Measurement, 51*(2), 393–402.

Gysbers, N. C., & Henderson, P. (2012). *Developing & managing your school guidance & counseling program.* Alexandria, VA: American Counseling Association.

Hatch, T. (2014). *The use of data in school counseling: Hatching results for students, programs and the profession.* Thousand Oaks, CA: Corwin.

Holcomb-McCoy, C. (2007). *School counseling to close the achievement gap: A social justice framework for success.* Thousand Oaks, CA: Corwin.

Hoover, H. D., Dunbar, S. B., & Frisbie, D. A. (2001). *Iowa test of basic skills.* Rolling Meadows, IL: Riverside Publishing.

Hutton, S. (2015, March). *Sustainability: The missing piece for long-term success.* Paper presented to the Third Annual National Evidence-Based School Counseling Conference, Highland Heights, KY. Retrieved from http://coehs.nku.edu/content/dam/coehs/docs/cfee/Sustainability%20Presentation%20_Steve%20Hutton.pdf

Kaffenberger, C., & Young, A. (2013). *Making data work* (3rd ed.). Alexandria, VA: American School Counselor Association.

Lapan, R. T., Gysbers, N. C., Stanley, B., & Pierce, M. E. (2012). Missouri professional school counselors: Ratios matter, especially in high-poverty schools. *Professional School Counseling, 16,* 108–116.

Lapan, R. T., Whitcomb, S. A., & Aleman, N. M. (2012). Connecticut professional school counselors: College and career counseling services and smaller ratios benefit students. *Professional School Counseling 16*, 117–124.

Lerner, R. M., Lerner, J. V., Almerigi, J. B., Theokas, C., Phelps, E., Gestsdottir, S., . . . von Eye, A. (2005). Positive youth development, participation in community youth development programs, and community contributions of fifth-grade adolescents: Findings from the first wave of the 4-H Study of Positive Youth Development. *The Journal of Early Adolescence, 25*(1), 17–71.

McDougal, J. L., Graney, S. B., Wright, J. A., & Ardoin, S. P. (2010). *RTI in practice: A practical guide to implementing effective evidence-based interventions in your school.* Hoboken, NJ: Wiley.

Myers, J. E., & Sweeney, T. J. (2005). *The five factor wellness inventory manual and sampler set, adult, teenage and elementary school versions.* Palo Alto, CA: Mind Garden.

Mynard, H., & Joseph, S. (2000). Development of the multidimensional peer-victimization scale. *Aggressive Behavior, 26*, 169–178.

Newman-Carlson, D., & Horne, A. M. (2004). Bully busters: A psycho-educational intervention for reducing bullying behavior in middle school students. *Journal of Counseling & Development, 82*, 259–268.

Orpinas, P., & Frankowski, R. (2001). The aggression scale: A self-report measure of aggressive behavior for young adolescents. *Journal of Early Adolescence, 21*(1), 50–67.

Orpinas, P., Horne, A. M., & Staniszewski, D. (2003). School bullying: Changing the problem by changing the school. *School Psychology Review, 32*(3), 431–444.

Sink, C. A., & Spencer, L. R. (2005). My Class Inventory-Short Form as an accountability tool for elementary school counselors to measure classroom climate. *Professional School Counseling, 9,* 37–48.

Sink, C. A., & Spencer, L. R. (2007). Teacher version of the My Class Inventory-Short Form: An accountability tool for elementary school counselors. *Professional School Counseling, 11,* 129–139. doi:10.5330/PSC.n.2010-11.129

Solberg, M., & Olweus, D. (2003). Prevalence estimation of school bullying with the Olweus Bully/Victim Questionnaire. *Aggressive Behavior, 29*, 239–268.

Sperling, R. A., Howard, B. C., Miller, L. A., & Murphy, C. (2002). Measures of children's knowledge and regulation of cognition. *Contemporary Educational Psychology, 27,* 51–79. doi:10.1006/ceps.2001.1091

Squier, K. L., Nailor, P., & Carey, J. C. (2014) *Achieving excellence in school counseling through motivation, self-direction, self-knowledge and relationships.* Thousand Oaks, CA: Corwin.

Stanford Achievement Test (10th ed.). (2012). Upper Saddle River, NJ: Pearson Assessment.

Stone, C. B., & Dahir, C. A. (2010). *School counselor accountability: A MEASURE of student success* (3rd ed.). Upper Saddle River, NJ: Pearson.

Villares, E., Frain, M., Brigman, G., Webb, L., & Peluso, P. (2012). The impact of Student Success Skills on standardized test scores: A meta-analysis. *Counseling Outcome Research and Evaluation, 3*(1), 3–16.

Index

Helping educators make the greatest impact

CORWIN HAS ONE MISSION: to enhance education through intentional professional learning.

We build long-term relationships with our authors, educators, clients, and associations who partner with us to develop and continuously improve the best evidence-based practices that establish and support lifelong learning.

The American School Counselor Association (ASCA) supports school counselors' efforts to help students focus on academic, college and career, and social/emotional development so they achieve success in school and are prepared to lead fulfilling lives as responsible members of society. ASCA, which is the school counseling division of the American Counseling Association, provides professional development, publications and other resources, research and advocacy to school counselors around the globe. For more information, visit www.schoolcounselor.org.